W9-BNM-436

335-1251

Old Baldy from Stockton Flats

C.W. McLaughlin

TRAILS
OF THE
ANGELES

100 Hikes in the San Gabriels

John W. Robinson

WILDERNESS PRESS
BERKELEY

First edition May 1971
Second edition May 1973
Third edition May 1976
Fourth edition March 1979
Fifth edition May 1984
Sixth edition January 1990
SEVENTH EDITION September 1998
Second printing January 2000
Third printing May 2001
Fourth printing June 2002

Photos by author except as noted
Cover photos: Rabbitbrush along the Angeles Crest Highway,
Bighorn sheep (inset), © 1998 by Roy Murphy

Book design by Terragraphics
Cover design by Jaan Hitt
Copyright © 1971, 1973, 1976, 1979, 1984, 1990, 1998 by John W. Robinson

Library of Congress Card Number 98-15475
ISBN 0-89997-232-2

Published by: **Wilderness Press**
1200 5th Street
Berkeley, CA 94710
(800) 443-7227; FAX (510) 558-1696
mail@wildernesspress.com

Contact us for free catalog
Visit our web site at **www.wildernesspress.com**

Printed on recycled paper

Library of Congress Cataloging-in-Publication Data
Robinson, John W.
   Trails of the Angeles : 100 hikes in the San Gabriels / John W. Robinson.
--7th ed.
      p.   cm.
   Includes bibliographical references (p.) and index.
   ISBN 0-89997-232-2 (alk. paper)
      1. Hiking--California--San Gabriel Mountains--Guidebooks. 2. San
   Gabriel Mountains (Calif.)--Guide-books.   I. Title.
   GV199.42.C22S277 1998
   917.94'93--dc21   98-15475
                                                                      CIP

All rights reserved. No part of this book may be reproduced in any form or
by any means without written permission from the publisher, with the excep-
tion of brief quotations for purposes of review.

Contents

Acknowledgments

It was the Long Beach Y.M.C.A. that introduced me to the San Gabriel Mountains, many years ago. As a boy, I spent many happy summer weeks at the Y's Kamp Kole on the West Fork of the San Gabriel River, hiking, fishing, camping under the stars, learning to know and love the mountains. Kamp Kole is gone now, but my gratitude remains. In more recent years, my friends in the Angeles Chapter of the Sierra Club have been my companions in the mountains and have introduced me to many of the delightful lesser-known trails of the range. Hiking the mountain trails and climbing the peaks generated a desire to learn more about the San Gabriels—their flora and fauna, their geology, their history. In satisfying this curiosity, I owe most to the late Will Thrall, editor of *Trails* magazine, who in his day knew more about the San Gabriels than any other man alive. Gratitude is also expressed to Dr. Edwin Carpenter and the Henry E. Huntington Library for providing access to the Will Thrall manuscripts and much other material on the mountains, to Guy Lewis and the Pasadena Historical Society, to the patient ladies of the Pasadena Public Library, and to many others who supplied valuable bits and pieces of information: Charles C. Vernon, William Mendenhall, Donald McLain, Elmer Smith, Odo Stade, Art DuFault, Eleanor Opid, Vint Hoegee, Kenyon DeVore, Anna and Norman Ross, Anselmo Lewis, Dick Worsfold, Gilbert Zepeda, and others. Without their help, this book would have been much less than what it is.

Keeping a guidebook up to date is a never-ending job, as, in the case of both humans and nature, change is constant. We have done our best to make the book as current as possible. Many thanks to Forest Service personnel—in particular Barbara Croonquist of the Mt. Baldy Ranger District and Gerald Reponen of the Chilao Visitor Center—and to the numerous hikers who have informed the author about trail and campground changes.

Russell Bell, Cary Green, Allan Klumpp, Anthony Sebestyen, Bruce Morrison, and Agnes Jaszenovics, all who have walked most of the trails in this book, provided invaluable help.

J.W.R.
Fullerton, California
November, 1999

Preface to the Seventh Edition

Twenty-seven years after initial publication, *Trails of The Angeles* continues to be a favorite of Southern California hikers, much to the author's gratification. Along with this appreciation, however, the author fully realizes his responsibility to keep the book up to date. Unlike a novel or even most books of nonfiction, a guidebook is really never completed. Change is constantly taking place, and the guidebook writer must be constantly alert to check out and record the changes.

In recent years, many changes have taken place in the San Gabriel Mountains, caused by a number of things: fire, flood, abandoning of old trails and campgrounds, building of new ones, and objections from private property owners whose land a road or trail may cross. Underlying many of these problems is the fact that the San Gabriels rise next door to one of the major population centers on the continent, which results in swarms of people using—and sometimes overusing—these mountains. Past editions have reflected many changes. This new edition contains the most changes of any.

The completion of the Pacific Crest Trail across the San Gabriels represents the biggest addition to Angeles trails in the past two decades. The upgrading of the Boy Scouts' 52-mile Silver Mocassin Trail from Chantry Flats to Mt. Baden-Powell offers hikers another possible cross-range jaunt. The setting aside of the 43,377-acre Sheep Mountain Wilderness in 1984 brings to three the number of wilderness areas in the San Gabriels, a total of 92,276 acres administered by the Forest Service in pristine condition.

In keeping with the new wilderness ethic, all the trail camps in the San Gabriel, Sheep Mountain, and Cucamonga wildernesses have been removed. Gone are such old favorites as Devils Canyon Trail Camp, the three trail camps in Bear Creek, Fish Fork and Iron Fork Trail Camps in the East Fork of the San Gabriel Canyon, and historic Kelly's Camp in the Cucamonga high country. In their place, without stoves or any other facilities, are what the author is calling "wilderness campsites"— places where one can lay out a sleeping bag amid nature unsullied with artificial trappings.

Another thing making it difficult to keep the book up-to-date is changing Forest Service regulations. A case in point is the wilderness permit system. As of this writing (January 1998), no wilderness permit is needed to enter San Gabriel Wilderness, a permit is needed to enter Sheep Mountain Wilderness only if you enter via the East Fork of San Gabriel Canyon, and a permit is required for *all* entry into Cucamonga Wilderness.

The Forest Service has been required to do some economic "belt tightening" in recent years. In the forests of Southern California, fire control takes first priority, and except for specially funded routes such as the Pacific Crest and Gabrielino trails, the Forest Service is no longer able to regularly maintain mountain trails. Many of these pathways would soon disappear in the fast-growing chaparral were it not for efforts by several volunteer hiking groups who care about the local mountains. Not only have these volunteers kept old trails in good condition, they have built new ones. The new San Gabriel Peak Trail (Trip 29), the so-called Mt. Zion Trail (Trip 43) and the Mt. Hawkins ridge trail (Trip 79) have all resulted from volunteer effort. Deserving special commendation for volunteer trail work are Charles Jones and the San Gabriel Mountains Trailbuilders; Roger Wells and "The Big Santa Anita Gang" Buddy Nichel and the Los Angeles Council of the Boy Scouts; Frank and Jean Nicholson, and Bill and Kathie Reilly, all of the JPL Hiking Club; Paul Ayers, Brian Marcroft, and John Harrigan of the Scenic Mt. Lowe Historical Committee; and of course "The Grand Old Man" of the Mount Wilson Trail, the late Ambrose Zaro. Thanks to the efforts of these individuals and groups, many historic pathways and several new ones are open to public enjoyment.

Introduction

*"There is no exercise so beneficial, physically, mentally, or
morally, nothing which gives so much of living for so little
cost, as hiking our mountain and hill trails and sleeping
under the stars."*

So wrote the late Will Thrall—explorer, historian, author, and protector
of the San Gabriel Mountains of Southern California.

Thrall's philosophy certainly applies today, in this age of high-pressure, rapid-paced urban life that engulfs so many Southern
Californians. Fortunately, there are mountains practically in the backyard of Los Angeles that offer the harried city-dweller a refreshing
change of pace. Here, amid forest, chaparral and stream, you can
redeem and revitalize yourself in nature's unhurried environment.
Traveling a wooded trail, scrambling along a rocky hillside, you can
find solitude and gain perspective; you will come to discover the true
value of wilderness to a civilization that too often places artificial values before real ones.

Over a century ago, in 1877, naturalist John Muir sampled the San
Gabriels, found them wild and trailless, and described the range as
"more rigidly inaccessible than any other I ever attempted to penetrate." Great change has come to the San Gabriels since Muir's excursion. This once-primitive high country he so vividly described in his
classic *Mountains of California* is today crisscrossed with paved highways, unpaved side roads, trails and fire breaks. Yet wilderness is here
for anyone who will leave behind pavement and camp ground and
seek it out on the numerous footpaths of the range.

This guidebook is a concerned effort to acquaint Southern
Californians with the intimate parts of the San Gabriels—the regions
away from highway and byway where nature still reigns relatively
undisturbed. One hundred hiking trips take the reader and prospective
hiker into almost every nook and cranny of the range. They vary from
easy one-hour strolls to all-day and overnight rambles involving many
miles of walking and much elevation change, from excursions that

should satisfy the novice to ones that challenge the veteran. For the history buff there are tours of the Mt. Lowe Railway and of the Echo Mountain ruins; for the nature lover, samplings of the San Gabriel and Cucamonga Wilderness areas, forever set aside in their natural state; for the "peak bagger," routes up all the major summits of the range.

The San Gabriels are laced with trails and fire roads—some well maintained and easy to follow, others almost-forgotten byways of the past, eroded and overgrown in spots. The great majority of trips in this guidebook are on maintained trails, and should offer no problems to the hiker. However, the writer has included a handful of cross-country excursions and trailless peak climbs in regions well worth visiting but not served by standard routes. For these trips, directions have been presented in greater detail. The writer has regretfully left out a few trips that were popular a few years ago, because the trails have become so badly overgrown as to be almost impassable. The Sturtevant and Tom Sloan trails are among these.

The writer has rewalked, recorded and researched all trips in this volume, most of them in recent years. Every effort has been made to present the information as accurately and as explicitly as possible. Nevertheless, the prospective hiker should be aware that several factors—some of them unique to the Southern California mountains—may make some of this information out of date in an amazingly short time. The first is the rapid growth of chaparral—the rigid, thorny brush that covers eighty percent of San Gabriel mountain slopes. A trail through this brushy maze, if not continually maintained, can become overgrown and virtually impassable in three years or less. Second is fire, the danger of which is extreme during late summer and fall, when the chaparral becomes tinder-dry. Fire denudes hillsides of vegetation, leaving them subject to dirt slippage and rockslides. Third is flood. Winter rainfall is generally moderate in the Southern California mountains (compared to the Sierra Nevada and other northern ranges), but every few years deluges occur that are particularly destructive to canyon trails. On fire-ravaged hillsides, water erosion can be severe, obliterating large sections of trail. Last is the continual reworking, regrading and rebuilding of maintained trails by the Forest Service and volunteer conservation groups. Sometimes part of a trail is relocated along a different route. Such changes will probably affect only a few of the trips described herein, but if you are unfamiliar with the area in which you plan to hike, it is best to inquire at a ranger station before the trip.

The trail trips have been graded, based on the writer's evaluation, as "easy," "moderate" or "strenuous." An "easy" trip is usually four miles or less in horizontal distance, with less than 500' elevation gain—suitable for beginners and children. A "moderate" trip—including the majority here—is a five-to-ten-mile hike, usually with less than 2500' elevation difference. You should be in fair physical condition for these, and children under 12 might find the going difficult. "Strenuous" trips are all-day rambles involving many miles of hiking and much elevation gain and loss; they are only for those in top physical condition and with hiking experience. The most important criteria for grading a trip were mileage covered, elevation gain and loss, and condition of the trail. Of less significance were accessibility of terrain, availability of water, exposure to sun, and ground cover. Obviously, some of the latter criteria depend on the weather and the time of year: a 3-mile hike over open chaparral slopes can be miserable under the hot August sun but delightful in January's cool breeze and cloudiness.

A season recommendation is also included for each trip. This classification is particularly important in the lower, south-facing parts of the range, where fire danger in summer and fall often reaches what the Forest Service calls "Stage One." During Stage One, campfires are permitted only in stoves in designated campgrounds and picnic areas. Gas-type portable stoves may be used if you obtain a California Campfire permit. In conditions of extreme fire danger, the forest may be closed to entry off of major highways.

To inquire about fire conditions, and for general questions concerning forest entry, you may contact one of the following Forest Service facilities:

Weekdays: Angeles National Forest headquarters (818) 574-1613
Arroyo Seco Ranger District (818) 790-1151
Tujunga Ranger District (818) 899-1900
Mt. Baldy Ranger District (626) 335-1251
Valyermo Ranger District (805) 944-2187
Saugus Ranger District (805) 296-9710
Lytle Creek Ranger Station (714) 887-2576

Weekends: Chilao Visitor Center (818) 796-5541
Big Pines Visitor Center (619) 249-3504
Crystal Lake Visitor Center (818) 910-1149
Mt. Baldy Visitor Center (909) 982-2829
Chantry Flats Information Station (818) 335-0712
San Gabriel Canyon Info. Station (626) 969-1012
Clear Creek Information Station (818) 797-9959
Littlerock Entrance Station (805) 944-2424

This book is entitled *Trails of the Angeles* because 95% of the San Gabriel Mountains are within Angeles National Forest. However, the eastern end of the range—from the great Baldy-Telegraph-Ontario

Ridge to Cajon Pass—is in San Bernardino National Forest. This section boasts some of the finest high country in the mountains, and it has been included because it belongs here better than with the topographically different San Bernardino Mountains several miles east. (See the author's *San Bernardino Mountain Trails* for 100 trips in the latter range.)

It is the writer's earnest desire that this guidebook will provide the prospective mountain visitor with the knowledge that can make an outing in the San Gabriels an enjoyable and meaningful experience. If you learn and heed forest regulations, follow route directions, become familiar with the area, have proper equipment, and use good sense, you will thoroughly appreciate your intimacy with the mountains. Never leave the trailhead without this preparation. The mountains are no place to travel alone, unbriefed, ill equipped or in poor condition. Enter their portals with the enthusiasm of adventure tempered with respect, forethought and common sense. The mountains belong to those who are wise as well as willing.

The San Gabriel Mountains

As long as humans have lived in the Los Angeles Basin, we have looked at the San Gabriel Mountains. Whether phantomlike behind a veil of brownish haze, sharply etched against a blue winter sky, or playing hide-and-seek with billowing clouds, they are a familiar scene on the northern skyline.

As mountains go, the San Gabriels are a gentle range. Ridgelines are sinuous rather than jagged, summits rounded rather than angular, slopes tapered rather than sheer. Although they present a formidable barrier to north-south travel, their elevations and topographical features do not compare with the sky-piercing crags of the Sierra Nevada.

The San Gabriels form a great roof over the Southern California coastal lowlands, covering an area that reaches from seaward slopes across to the Mojave Desert, and extends west-to-east 63 miles from the Ridge Route to Cajon Pass. It can be said that the mountains act as both hero and villain to the Southland's millions: they protect the coastal plains from the desert's harshness and gather moisture from Pacific storms, but at the same time increase urban air pollution by locking in air masses.

Geologists tell us the range is a massive block of the earth's crust, separated from the surrounding landscape by a network of major faults—the San Andreas Fault on the north, the San Gabriel and Sierra Madre faults on the south, and the Soledad Fault on the west. The great block itself, in turn, is fractured by numerous subsidiary faults. The result is a surface that is extremely uneven. Eons of erosive stream action have cut deep V-shaped canyons, further accentuating the unevenness. The surface rocks are fractured and intermixed in great confusion, forming a heterogeneous mixture of crystalline limestone, schists and quartzites, which have been invaded by intrusive granites and other igneous rocks, all forming a most complicated mass.

Covering about 80% of this wrinkled mountain mass is a thick blanket of stiff, thorny shrubs and dwarf trees collectively called chaparral: chamise, scrub oak, yucca, wild lilac, mountain mahogany, laurel, snowbrush (whitethorn), chinquapin, and that unpopular champion of all rigidity, manzanita. This elfin forest, where it has not recently been burned off—for it grows quickly back—fastens securely to hillsides, seizing every square foot not pre-empted by timber or crag. It swarms over hot, exposed slopes whose conditions it alone can endure, spreading until it forms an almost impenetrable collar between the foothills and the high pine country.

Chaparral has been damned as "too low to give shade, too high to see over, and too thick to go through." Anyone so foolish as to venture off road or trail and crawl through this brushy maze will soon come to believe there is a personal hostility in the unyielding branches and scratchy leaves.

A different experience awaits those who consider this elfin forest as a friend to visit, not as an enemy to thrash through. In bloom, much of

Jerry Schad

The San Gabriel Mountains

the chaparral is sprinkled with colorful flowers. And what is more pleasing to the nature lover than ceanothus blooming into misty blue or white, California laurel unfolding masses of yellow flowers, or wild lilac giving forth its sweet aroma after a spring rain? Chaparral is also valuable as a soil cover; where it has been burned off, rain rushes down the hillsides, causing severe erosion on the slopes and flooding in the canyons.

Below the chaparral belt, in the canyons, a luxuriant cover of sycamore, live oak, alder and bay shields sparkling streams from the sun's glare. Above the chaparral, and sometimes as enclaves within it, is a cool, stately world of conifers: first big-cone spruce; then—progressively higher—Jeffrey and ponderosa pine, Coulter pine, incense-cedar, sugar pine, white fir, and lodgepole pine. On the highest ridges, subalpine conditions reign, and gnarled limber pines live a marginal existence among windswept crags.

The wildlife of the San Gabriel Mountains is timid—as well it should be. Humans have pre-empted most of the range, crowding out animals that once roamed in abundance. Some species are gone completely: no longer does the giant California condor soar overhead, nor the mammoth grizzly bear prowl the forest. Both disappeared from here shortly after the turn of the century. Rarely seen in the San Gabriels is the black bear; naturalists estimate that 150 are left, and the number is decreasing. In the remote recesses of the range, about 400 Nelson bighorn sheep scratch out a living. You must walk far from the highway to see these noble animals, deep into the rugged San Gabriel and Cucamonga wildernesses or high up on the stony battlements of Iron Mountain.

The most abundant large mammal in the San Gabriels is the California mule deer, usually yellow-brown in summer, gray in winter, its many-pronged antlers growing to considerable size. Preying on the deer are a growing number of mountain lions, perhaps 40 or 50 in the whole range. In recent years, sightings of these agile beasts have increased, and their large and unmistakable track is often seen on the trail. (Small children should not be left unattended in the mountains.) Smaller mammals include the bobcat, ring-tailed cat, gray fox, weasel, skunk, and a host of squirrels and chipmunks. The region's only creature considered sometimes dangerous to humans is the western rattlesnake, abundant below 6000', and sometimes seen up to 8000'. However, most rattlers are not very aggressive, and will crawl away when approached.

Geographically, the San Gabriels are for most of their length made up of two roughly parallel ranges. The northern, inland range is the longer and loftier, extending from Mt. Gleason and Mt. Pacifico eastward past the 8000' and 9000' summits of Waterman, Williamson, Islip,

Hawkins, Throop and Baden-Powell, and climaxing near its eastern end in the only summit over 10,000'—Mt. San Antonio (Old Baldy) and its cluster of satellite peaks. The southern, or front, range, though neither as long nor as high, is equally as rugged. Two of its summits—Strawberry and San Gabriel—exceed 6000', and 10 others exceed 5000'. Below the peaks is a complex of deep, shaded canyons, extending well up into the higher parts of the range. The range's major watershed is the San Gabriel River, whose three main forks and countless tributaries drain fully 20% of the mountain precipitation. Other important watersheds are Pacoima, Little and Big Tujunga, Arroyo Seco, Santa Anita, San Antonio and Lytle Creek canyons on the south slope of the range, and Little Rock and Big Rock creeks on the north.

Finally, there is the Liebre Mountain-Sawmill Mountain-Sierra Pelona country to the northwest of the San Gabriels proper, beyond the great wind gap of Soledad Canyon. Geographers disagree on whether this gentle mountain region of long whaleback ridges and shallow canyons belongs to the San Gabriels, to the Tehachapis, or to neither. But it is part of Angeles National Forest and it is good hiking country, so it is included here.

Other mountain ranges in California are higher, more jagged, more bedecked with ice and snow, more breathtaking, more primitive. But no other is so accessible to so many people for so little effort—and year-around. When winter's white mantle closes off the high country, the woodsy canyons and green-velvet foothills become refreshing, delightful and inviting. And then, in turn, when summer's sweltering dryness invades canyon and foothill, the high mountains once again beckon. For this all-season aspect, and for the San Gabriels themselves—ageless, rock-ribbed, aromatic with the restoring scents of forest and chaparral—shall we ever be thankful.

Humans in the San Gabriels

Humans have entered the San Gabriels in almost every conceivable manner. We have come into the mountains for a multitude of reasons. And we have come in great numbers. Few mountain ranges anywhere have been so much viewed, swarmed over, dug into, and built upon by the human species.

What draws us to the mountains? Is it curiosity? The promise of adventure? The excitement of hunting and fishing? The chance of a better livelihood? The quest for mineral wealth? The longing to redeem and revitalize oneself, away from the hustle of urban life? The need for something spiritual or ego-satisfying? The long pageant of humans in the San Gabriels reveals all these motives. along with some that are not so readily identified. The fascination of the canyons, the ridges. the peaks, the little flats that lie deep in the mountains, has attracted human visitors since humans first made their home in Southern California. Humans have come to the mountains, have seen, have lingered, and in many cases have remained for life.

One might suppose that the San Gabriels would be worn out (ecologically) by all this human activity. Some parts are, particularly in the front range. Fortunately, though, there are other areas where human impact has been minimal, where nature still rules—thanks to the protective efforts of a handful of people who, for a variety of reasons ranging from enlightened self-interest to esthetic values, have fought to save the mountains and the forests for the benefit of all. Humankind is not totally shortsighted although we often appear to be.

The first humans in the San Gabriels were Indian peoples of Shoshonean stock—Gabrielinos in the southern foot hills, Fernandenos in the western canyons. and Serranos in the eastern and northern high country.* Although their homes were generally below the mountains,

---

* These tribal names were assigned by anthropologists. The groups named *Gabrielinos* and *Fernandos* were associated with Missions San Gabriel and San Fernando, respectively. *Serrano* is derived from the Spanish word meaning "mountaineer." Other tribal groups in the Liebre-Sawmill-Sierra Pelona country were the Alliklik and the Kitanemuk peoples, also Shoshonean.

these peoples depended heavily on the San Gabriels. The mountains supplied them with food, water and materials for building and hunting. For food, they hunted deer and rabbit, and gathered acorns and pine nuts. Water they took from the streams that gushed down from the heights. Chaparral was an abundant source of many necessities. Manzanita berries were pressed for cider, and the leaves were smoked. Greasewood provided arrow shafts for hunting. Yucca fibers were used to make nets and ropes.

To obtain these materials, and to visit and trade with other peoples across the range, Indians made the first footpaths into the mountains. According to Will Thrall, foremost collector of San Gabriel Mountains history, who personally searched out these ancient routes at a time when they could still be followed, the main Shoshone trail across the range ascended Millard Canyon, traversed behind Mt. Lowe to Red Box Saddle, descended the West Fork of the San Gabriel River to Valley Forge Canyon, climbed up that canyon to Barley Flats, went down and across the head of Big Tujunga Canyon and up to Pine (Charlton) Flat, and continued on to the west end of Chilao. Here the trail forked. One branch followed the high country northeast to Buckhorn, then went down the South Fork of Little Rock Creek to the desert. The other branch dropped northwest into upper Alder Creek, then ascended Indian Ridge (where traces of the old footpath can still be seen) to Sheep Camp Spring on the west slope of Mt. Pacifico, and dropped down Santiago Canyon to Little Rock Creek and along it to the desert. Another cross-range trail ascended the North Fork of the San Gabriel River, climbed over Windy Gap, and descended the South Fork of Big Rock Creek to the desert. For perhaps two or three centuries before the arrival of the white settlers, these and many shorter canyon trails were trod by hundreds of Indians every year.

The coming of the Spaniards was to change life in the pleasant valleys below the mountains forever. In 1771, along the grassy banks of the Rio Hondo, Mission San Gabriel Arcangel was founded, and soon thereafter the Gabrielinos were incorporated into the mission community. Mission San Fernando Rey de Espana, founded in 1797, became the home of the less-numerous Fernandenos. At the height of mission activity—around 1800—these two outposts of the cross numbered some 2000 Indians in their widespread flocks.

Several decades later came the era of the great ranchos, bringing a pastoral way of life to the valleys. These spacious cattle ranches that spread out below the south slopes of the range bore the familiar names of San Fernando, Tujunga, La Canada, San Pascual, Santa Anita, Azusa de Duarte, and San Jose.

The Spanish and Mexican Californios used the mountains very little except as a source of water. When there were buildings to be constructed, woodcutters sometimes took timber from the lower canyons. Vaqueros did some hunting in the canyons and foothills. Grizzly bears, numerous in the range then, were stalked and captured, then dragged to the bull ring in the Pueblo of Los Angeles to be sacrificed in brutal bear-bull contests.

There is no evidence that the Spaniards ever penetrated into the heart of the mountains, although they certainly explored the fringes. Gaspar de Portola and Pedro Fages, on their epic journey northward in 1769, toiled through the "narrow canyon" of San Fernando Pass and found "high, barren hills, very difficult for beasts of burden" before dropping into pleasant Newhall Valley. Fages in 1772, on another pathfinding trip, crossed the eastern end of the range in the vicinity of Cajon Pass and continued northwest below the northern ramparts of the mountains, discovering the Joshua trees. Fray Francisco Garces, the missionary-explorer-martyr, explored both sides of the range in 1776. Fray Jose Maria Zalvidea in 1806 almost circled what is now Angeles National Forest.

It was the Spaniards who gave the mountains their name—two names, in fact, that have existed side by side down to recent years. Garces in 1776 referred to the range as "Sierra de San Gabriel," borrowing the name of the nearby mission, and this name was used in Spanish records frequently in ensuing years. But the mission padres usually referred to the range as "Sierra Madre" ("Mother Range"). Both "San Gabriel" and "Sierra Madre" were in common usage until 1927, when the United States Board on Geographic Names finally ruled in favor of the former. Today, "San Gabriel Mountains" is almost universally accepted.

With the coming of the Anglos—from the 1840s onward—the San Gabriels began to receive more attention. Prospectors, hunters, bandits, homesteaders and squatters were the pioneers in unveiling the secrets of the mountains. These hardy individuals first entered the wooded canyons, then forged their way over the ridges and into the hidden heart of the range—terrain the rancheros had scorned.

Stories of gold in the San Gabriels go back as far as the 1770s, but not until 1842, when Francisco Lopez discovered gold clinging to the roots of a cluster of wild onions in Placerita Canyon, near present-day Newhall, was there what might be called a gold rush. The San Fernando Placers, as the discovery was called, were worked on and off for about a decade, until strikes elsewhere drew the miners away. By far the largest gold strike in the San Gabriels occurred on the East Fork of the San Gabriel River. The precious metal was discovered in the canyon gravels in 1854, and for the next seven years the East Fork was the scene of frenzied activity, an estimated $2 million in gold being recovered. A smaller strike occurred in Big Santa Anita Canyon about the same time. During the next half century, prospectors rushed into the mountains at every rumor of bonanza, tearing up hillsides in their frantic search for wealth.

Bandits, including Jack Powers, Salmon Pico, Juan Flores, and the legendary Tiburcio Vasquez, turned to the San Gabriels for refuge. They drove stolen cattle and horses up the canyons and pastured them in back-country flats. Utilizing the faint network of old Indian trails, these outlaws established isolated hideouts deep in the mountains.

The pioneer trail-builder in the San Gabriels was Benjamin Wilson, who in 1864 reworked an old Indian path up Little Santa Anita Canyon to the top of the mountain that now bears his name. During the next three decades, trails were blazed up all the major canyons of the front range, some of them continuing over the ridges and into the back country. In increasing numbers, homesteaders and squatters followed these trails and found favorite spots on which to build their cabins. The names of many of these early mountain men have come down to the present, attached to canyons, camps and peaks—Wilson, Millard, Henninger, Newcomb, Chantry, Chilao, Islip and Dawson, to name a few.

Almost all these pioneers came into the mountains for utilitarian reasons—to mine gold, to cut timber, to find refuge, to pasture livestock, to establish a home. Around 1885 a new reason for going to the mountains arose—recreation. Great numbers of San Gabriel Valley residents journeyed to Mt. Wilson on weekends and holidays to enjoy the cool mountain air and take in the fabulous panorama. (This was before air pollution muddled Southland skies.) Hunters entered the range seeking big game, plentiful in the San Gabriels until around the turn of the century. Grizzly bear, black bear, deer, mountain sheep and mountain lion were stalked by bands of thrill-seeking hunters who penetrated far into the mountains. Sportsmen packed in for a week's fishing on the trout-filled West Fork of the San Gabriel River. For the less energetic, there were Sunday afternoon picnics in such woodsy haunts as Millard and Eaton canyons.

Other people entered the mountains for a different reason—exploitation. Most Americans of that day assumed that our natural resources were inexhaustible and therefore there was no need to conserve them. Lumber was needed to fuel Southern California's great boom of the 1880s; why not use the timber close at hand? Indiscriminate cutting of forest trees appeared imminent. Furthermore, the value of chaparral for the mountain watershed was little understood. Brush fires, some deliberately set by cattlemen to clear land for grazing, raged across the mountains until extinguished by rain. Fortunately, some farsighted citizens in Los Angeles and the San Gabriel Valley became alarmed at this exploitation and devastation of the local mountains, and began working to preserve them.

One of these was Abbott Kinney, a rancher, botanist and land developer who lived at his Kinneloa Ranch above Altadena. Kinney is best remembered as the creator of Venice, the Southern California beach town that once had canals for streets, but it was as chairman of California's first Board of Forestry that he did his most important work. In the first report of the Board of Forestry to Governor Stoneman in 1886, Kinney urged "intelligent supervision of the forest land and brush lands of California, with a view to their preservation." This California movement for forest conservation, sparked by Kinney and others, soon became part of a national movement. John Muir, using his eloquence in a series of magazine articles urging forest protection, was the leading spokesman.

Congress finally responded by passing the Forest Reserve Act of 1891, granting the President authority "to set aside as public reservations public lands bearing forest wholly or in part covered with timber or undergrowth." As a result of this act, and strong pressure from Southern California civic leaders, President Benjamin Harrison signed the bill establishing the San Gabriel Timberland Reserve on December 20, 1892. This was the first forest reserve in California, and the second in the United States.[*] The designation was at first rather ineffectual; for one thing, forest rangers were not assigned until 1898. But gradually the San Gabriel Timberland Reserve was brought under efficient forest management and protection. In 1907 the name was changed to "San Gabriel National Forest," and the following year it became what we know today—"Angeles National Forest." A succession of capable supervisors—Everett Thomas, Theodore Lukens, Rush Charlton, William Mendenhall, Sim Jarvi, William Dresser and Paul Sweetland—have made the Angeles one of the most effectively run national forests in the nation.

Worldwide fame came to the San Gabriels in the 1890s with construction of the Mt. Lowe Scenic Railway, considered one of the engineering wonders of its time. This breathtaking cable incline and trolley ride, along with associated hotels in Rubio Canyon, atop Echo Mountain, and on the slopes of Mt. Lowe, was the brain child of inventor Thaddeus Lowe and engineer David Macpherson. The famed mountain railway-resort complex attracted over three million visitors during its 43 years of operation.

The human quest for scientific knowledge played its part in the story of the mountains too. In the days before city lights and air pollution interfered with sky-viewing, Mt. Wilson's broad summit was ideal for astronomical observation. The first telescope on Mt. Wilson was the

---

[*] First was the Yellowstone Park Timberland Reserve in Wyoming, established by Presidential proclamation on September 16, 1891.

13-incher of Harvard University Observatory, placed on the summit in 1889 (but removed the following year). 1904 saw the beginning of the Carnegie Institute's famed Mt. Wilson Observatory, one of the 20th century's great scientific ventures. Largely through the initiative and enthusiasm of astronomer George Ellery Hale, several of the world's greatest telescopes were erected on the mountaintop, the most important being the 60" reflector (1908), the 150' solar tower telescope (1912), and the 100" Hooker reflector (1917), the latter the world's largest optical telescope for 31 years.

Before highways crisscrossed the San Gabriels, the mountains were the delight of hikers. During the period from about 1895 to 1938 there occurred what mountain historians call the Great Hiking Era. Multitudes of lowland residents enjoyed their weekends and holidays rambling over the range. Trails that today are almost deserted vibrated to the busy tramp of boots and the merry singing of hikers. The mountains were a local frontier for exploration and a challenge to the hardy. For some, hiking was simply a favorite sport; for others, it was almost a religion. Trail resorts sprang up to offer hospitality, food and lodging to hikers. Such places as Switzer's, Opid's, Colby's, Loomis', Sturtevant's and Roberts' were visited by thousands every season.

A strange combination of disasters and "progress" brought the Great Hiking Era to a close. The disasters were a series of fires and consequent floods, the great destructive torrent of March 1938 being the final blow. Overnight, miles of canyon trails were obliterated. "Progress" took the form of the Angeles Crest Highway, begun in 1929. Relentlessly, the great asphalt thoroughfare snaked its way into the heart of the mountains, reaching Red Box in 1934, Charlton Flat in 1937, and Chilao a year later. By 1941 it had inched its way across Cloudburst Summit and reached that most isolated of back-country haunts, Buckhorn. Places that once required a day or two of strenuous hiking now were accessible in an hour of driving. One by one, the old trail resorts succumbed. As one old-timer sadly reflected, "Only people who hike for the love of hiking use these trails now." The Angeles Crest Highway, more than anything else, changed the pattern of our use of the San Gabriels.

In recent years, great numbers of people have visited the San Gabriels, the vast majority by automobile, and visitation is increasing. In 1945 Angeles National Forest visitors numbered an estimated 1,310,000. In 1988 the figure had swollen to about 32,000,000, making the Angeles the second most heavily used national forest in the United States.

As the use has increased, the wilderness aspect of the mountains has been nearly destroyed. Other than the specially set aside San Gabriel, Cucamonga and Sheep Mountain wilderness areas and a few other small, isolated regions, the San Gabriels have in recent years become not much more than a king-sized backyard playground for Los Angeles County. Some say this is as it should be, but recent ecological studies have tended to show that wilderness undisturbed by humans plays a vital part in nature's delicate balance among living things. What happens when there is no wilderness left? Southern California appears headed in that direction.

Angeles National Forest today encompasses 693,667 acres. Within this mountain area are 988 miles of roads, 775 miles of riding and hiking trails, 89 public campgrounds, 43 picnic areas, 8 resorts, 24 organizational camps, 707 summer residences, and 6 winter sports areas.

The future of the San Gabriels—as well as all other mountain ranges—rests with the population that lives nearby. In the words of mountain historian Charles Clark Vernon, "They are truly a gift to the people." What the people will do with this gift of nature remains to be seen.

Mountain Courtesy

Traveling a mountain trail, away from centers of civilization, is a unique experience in Southern California living. It brings intimate association with nature—communion with the earth, the forest, the chaparral, the wildlife, the clear sky. A great responsibility accompanies this experience—the obligation to keep the mountains as you found them. Being considerate of the wilderness rights of others will make the mountain adventures of those who follow equally rewarding.

As a mountain visitor, you should become familiar with the rules of wilderness courtesy outlined below.

Trails

Never cut switchbacks. This practice breaks down trails and hastens erosion. Take care not to dislodge rocks that might fall on hikers below you. Improve and preserve trails, as by clearing away loose rocks (carefully) and removing branches. Report any trail damage and broken or misplaced signs to a ranger.

Off Trail

Restrain the impulse to blaze trees or to build ducks where not essential. Let the next fellow find his way as you did.

Mountain Bikes

Mountain bikers need to respect the rights and the safety of hikers and horseback riders, and to follow sound conservation practices. Yield right-of-way to other trail users. Control your speed. Stay off muddy trails, and do not shortcut switchbacks. Mountain biking is permissible on most forest trails but is prohibited in wilderness areas and on the Pacific Crest Trail.

Campgrounds

Spread your gear in an already-cleared area, and build your fire in a campground stove. Don't disarrange the camp by making hard-to-eradicate ramparts of rock for fireplaces or windbreaks. Rig tents and tarps with line tied to rocks or trees; never put nails in trees. For your campfire, use fallen wood only; do not cut standing trees nor break off branches. Use the campground latrine. Place litter in the litter can or carry it out. Leave the campground cleaner than you found it.

Fire

Fire is the greatest danger in the Southern California mountains; act accordingly. Smoking is permitted only in campgrounds, places of habitation, and vehicles. Report a mountain fire immediately to the Forest Service.

Litter

Along the trail, place candy wrappers, raisin boxes, orange peels, etc. in your pocket or pack for later disposal; throw nothing on the trail. Pick up litter you find along the trail or in camp. More than almost anything else, litter detracts from the wilderness scene. Remember, you can take it with you.

Noise

Boisterous conduct is out of harmony in a wilderness experience. Be a considerate hiker and camper. Don't ruin another's enjoyment of the mountains.

Good Samaritanship

Human life and well-being take precedence over everything else— in the mountains as elsewhere. If a hiker or camper is in trouble, help in any way you can. Indifference is a moral crime. Give comfort or first aid; then hurry to a ranger station for help.

Maps

It is important to know where you are in relation to roads, campgrounds, landmarks, etc. and to have a general understanding of the lay of the land. For this orientation there is no substitute for a good map. Unless your trip is very short, and over a well-marked route, you should carry a map.

There are two types of maps readily available that will give you the picture you need of the San Gabriel Mountains. Each type has its advantages and disadvantages.

1. The U.S. Forest Service sells recreation maps of each national forest for a small sum. For the San Gabriels, you will need the maps of Angeles and San Bernardino national forests. These maps show the highways, dirt roads, maintained trails, campgrounds, and major landmarks of the range, but not the topography. Their main advantages are that they give you an overall picture of the mountains and are fairly up-to-date, being revised frequently. Since they don't show topographic features or ground cover, they are virtually useless for cross-country travel. These maps can be obtained at most ranger stations in the two national forests. Or write to the forest headquarters:

Angeles National Forest
701 N. Santa Anita
Arcadia, CA 91006
(818) 574-1613

San Bernardino National Forest
1824 Commercenter Circle
San Bernardino, CA 92408
(909) 383-5588

2. If you do much hiking, particularly cross country, you will want to use topographic ("topo") maps, because they afford accurate information about the topography and the forest or brush cover. Topo maps

are available in several sizes and scales, but the best for the San Gabriels, because they are the most up-to-date and show the greatest detail, are the U.S. Geological Survey's 7.5-minute topographic quadrangle series. Their scale is approximately 2½ inches to a mile; the contour interval (elevation difference between contour lines) is 40' and the area covered by each map is about 7 × 9 miles. They show most maintained and many unmaintained trails, elevations, relief, watercourses, forest and brush cover, and works of man. Learning to "read" these maps takes some practice, but the savings in shoe leather and frayed temper make it a worthwhile undertaking. Twenty-seven topo maps (in the 7.5' series) cover the San Gabriel Mountains. The appropriate topo map(s) for each trip is cited in the trip heading. Topo maps can be bought at many sporting goods and mountaineering-ski shops. Or write to the Geological Survey's Western Distribution Center:

U.S. Geological Survey
Federal Center
Denver, CO 80225

. . . or order from Wilderness Press' retail map store:

The Map Center
2440 Bancroft Way
Berkeley, CA 94704
(510) 841-6277

They will fill phone orders.

Important!

A Forest Adventure Permit is required to park in any of the four national forests in Southern California. $30 for an annual pass; $5 for a day pass. The Adventure Pass can be purchased at ranger stations, visitor centers, and many business establishments in or near the mountains.

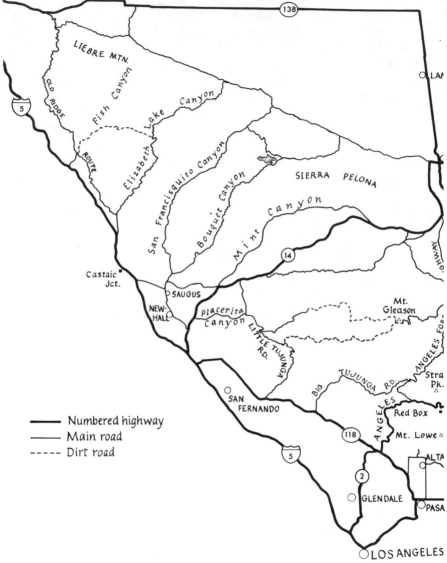

Numbered highway
Main road
----- Dirt road

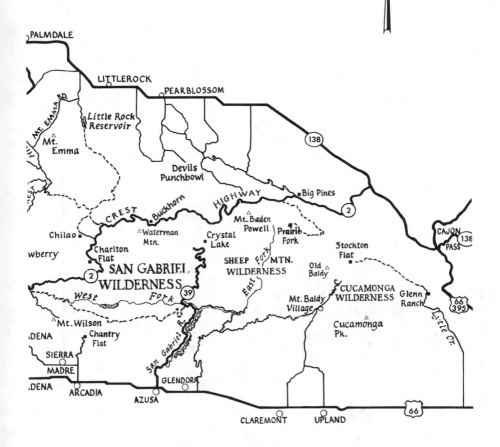

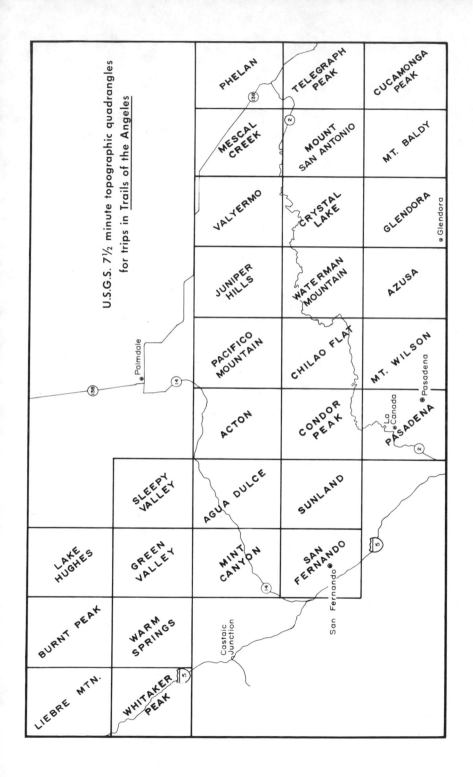

U.S.G.S. 7½ minute topographic quadrangles for trips in Trails of the Angeles

PHELAN | TELEGRAPH PEAK | CUCAMONGA PEAK

MESCAL CREEK | MOUNT SAN ANTONIO | MT. BALDY

VALYERMO | CRYSTAL LAKE | GLENDORA

JUNIPER HILLS | WATERMAN MOUNTAIN | AZUSA

PACIFICO MOUNTAIN | CHILAO FLAT | MT. WILSON

ACTON | CONDOR PEAK | PASADENA

SLEEPY VALLEY | AGUA DULCE | SUNLAND

LAKE HUGHES | GREEN VALLEY | MINT CANYON | SAN FERNANDO

BURNT PEAK | WARM SPRINGS

LIEBRE MTN. | WHITAKER PEAK

Palmdale

Glendora

Pasadena

La Canada

Castaic Junction

San Fernando

One Hundred Hikes

The hiking trips in this guide are arranged by geographical area, generally west to east. Thus, trips 1-4 are in the Liebre-Sawmill-Sierra Pelona country at the western end of the range. Since the front range of the San Gabriels has the greatest number of trails and fire roads, this section has the greatest number of trips: 5-48. Trips 49-70 explore the back country from the West Fork of the San Gabriel River over the crest of the range to the desert. The middle high country—the mountains above the North and East forks of the San Gabriel—is covered in trips 71-89. Trips 90-100 are in the eastern high country—from Mt. San Antonio to the eastern end of the range.

Information about each trip is divided into three parts: *Trip, Features,* and *Description.*

The *Trip* section gives vital statistics: where the hike starts and ends; the walking mileage and elevation gain or loss; a rating of easy, moderate or strenuous; the best time of year to make the trip; and the appropriate USGS topographic map or maps.

The *Features* section tells something of what you will see on the trip, and gives information on the natural and human history of the area. It also contains suggestions for the particular trip, such as: wear lug-soled boots, or bring fishing rod.

The *Description* section details driving and hiking routes. The driving directions are kept to the necessary minimum, while the walking route is described in detail. Also, hiking options that a trip presents are described.

If you are a dedicated hiker who enjoys exploring the San Gabriels on foot, the trips listed here are just a beginning. Many more than 100 hikes are possible in the San Gabriels, crisscrossed as these mountains are by walking routes. Furthermore, various combinations of routes described here are possible, particularly if you can arrange car shuttles. You could spend a decade rambling through the range and still not totally know the mountains.

1 County Road N2 via Horse Trail to Liebre Mountain

HIKE LENGTH:	6 miles round trip; 1700' elevation gain
CLASSIFICATION:	Moderate
SEASON:	All year
TOPO MAP:	Liebre Mountain

Features

The long whaleback of Liebre Mountain sprawls at the northwest corner of Angeles National Forest, where the Coast Ranges, the Tehachapis and the San Gabriels all meld together in a wrinkled jumble. From Liebre's broad summit, you look north across golden-brown Antelope Valley to the Tehachapis, curving from west to northeast in a great arc; and if the day is clear, the southern ramparts of the Sierra Nevada are visible on the distant skyline. Southward, you peer into the gentle ridge-and-canyon country of the Cienaga and Fish Canyon watersheds.

This is delightful mountain country, especially in spring, when snow patches linger on north slopes, the California black oak is clothing itself with reddish leaves, and aromatic white sage is blooming in the foothills. This is the home of the digger pine, hardy dweller on semi-arid slopes, easily identifiable by its gray-green needles, its large cones (second in size only to the Coulter pine), and its multi-forked trunk. Also on the mountainside are big-cone spruce and some rather large scrub oak. Occasional junipers and pinyon pines bear testimony to the blending of mountain and desert here.

This trip follows the historic old Horse Trail, now part of the Pacific Crest Trail system, but once used to drive horses from the Tejon Ranch to Los Angeles, steeply up the forested north slope of Liebre Mountain from Horse Trail Flat to the summit. Do it in leisurely fashion, to fully appreciate the desert view and the unique combination of forest trees and chaparral. It's a long drive from Los Angeles, but the mountainside is remote, peaceful and beautiful—well worth the effort.

Description

From Interstate 5, 4 miles south of Gorman, turn east onto State Highway 138. After 4½ miles turn right (southeast) onto the Old Ridge Route. Follow the latter 2½ miles, then turn left (east) onto County Road N2. Drive this road 4.2 miles, to a high point just before the road begins to descend. Turn right (south) and drive on dirt tracks about 100 feet to the oak-shaded parking area.

At the upper edge of the parking area is the Pacific Crest Trail, the southbound section climbing west, the northbound dropping southeast. Take the southbound PCT, which ascends the mountainside. (If you start descending you're on the wrong trail segment.) You switch-

Black oak with mistletoe, Liebre Mountain

back up through live oaks and digger pines, with far-ranging views over Antelope Valley to the Tehachapis. After 2 miles you pass Wilderness Camp to your right. There are a table and a fire ring here but no water. (Water can usually be found in Horse Camp Canyon just behind and steeply down from the camp; the easiest way to get water is to continue up the trail a quarter-mile, where the descent into the canyon is less steep.) You continue switchbacking upward, under a cool canopy of pine and oak. Near the top your trail becomes an old jeep track. About 60 yards before you reach the crest and a junction with Forest Road 7N23, turn right and scramble to the small rock cairn that marks the 5791-foot summit of Liebre Mountain.

Return the way you came. Or, with a car shuttle, meet your transportation on Forest Road 7N23 on the crest of the long Liebre hogback. To drive to the crest, follow the Old Ridge Route to its crossing of the west end of Liebre Mountain, 5 miles up from State Highway 138, then turn left (east) onto 7N23. Follow the latter, a narrow dirt road, steep in places, to the crest. ▲

2 Sawmill Mountain Ridge to Atmore Meadows, Gillette Mine, Bear Canyon

HIKE LENGTH:	14 miles round trip; 1700' elevation loss and gain
CLASSIFICATION:	Moderate to Strenuous
SEASON:	All year
TOPO MAPS:	Burnt Peak, Liebre Mountain

Features

Just south of the great whalebacks of Liebre and Sawmill mountains lies some of the loneliest mountain country in Angeles National Forest. This is a region of long, meandering canyons, gentle ridges, and rounded summits. Chaparral is king here; its prickly greenness blankets everything except the canyon bottoms, where tall oaks and sycamores grow and there are a few isolated stands of spruce and pine. This is also the realm of California mule deer, a favorite of hunters. Hikers are rare, yet the country has a multitude of trails. Unfortunately, many of them are presently overgrown, no longer maintained by the Forest Service. You must be prepared for some bushwacking, and a few spots where the trail is so overgrown that it is difficult to follow. This trip is not recommended for beginning hikers.

This trip begins near Atmore Meadows, contours over slopes of scrub oak, manzanita, yucca, and chamise and its cousin red shanks, then drops into Bear Canyon. (There are three Bear Canyons in the Angeles.) Here you visit the ruins of the Gillette Mine, a gold-and-silver prospect dating from the 1880s. Enroute you pass several trail junctions, each offering opportunities for further discovery (see Description below). The best time of year is spring, when there is still water in the canyons, when oaks and sycamores are dressing themselves in red and green, and when the air is sweet with the perfume of wet chaparral. Autumn is crisp and dry, yet the leaves of the black oak on Sawmill Mountain—some yellow, some almost bright red—produce a vivid splash of color against the drab background.

Description

From Interstate 5, 4 miles south of Gorman, turn right (east) onto State Highway 138. After 4½ miles turn right again (southeast) onto the Old Ridge Route. About 2½ miles farther turn left (east) onto County Road N2. Follow N2 13 miles to Bushnell Summit, where it intersects Forest Road 7N23 leading right (southwest) up Sawmill Mountain. Follow 7N23 to the crest of the mountain, 3 miles, then right (west) along the ridgetop 3½ more miles to the intersection with the Atmore Meadows spur road, 7N19. Park here.

Walk around the locked gate and follow 7N19 down to a horseshoe bend just short of the abandoned Atmore Meadows campground, 2 miles.

The trail leads south from this horseshoe bend in the road, passes a seepage, and in ½ mile reaches a junction. The left fork descends into Fish Canyon (see Trip 3). Go right, across chaparral slopes to a prominent saddle. Here the trail, much of it overgrown, contours along the side of the ridge, and climbs slightly before descending into Bear Canyon, 4 miles from 7N19. It's easy to miss a switchback here, thanks to overgrown chaparral, so proceed carefully.

In Bear Canyon you meet a dirt road coming over the ridge from Knapp Ranch. Go left and follow the road down-canyon ½ mile to the Gillette Mine remains, marked by tailings and rusted metal. Across the creek is a more recent mine owned by the Benco Mining Company, not being developed as of this writing (November 1999).

Return the same way, almost all uphill. You have the option of continuing down Bear Canyon to its merger with Cienaga Canyon, 3 miles. However, the old trail has largely disappeared and you must follow the creek and negotiate some brushy areas. Unfortunately, the once scenic trail over Redrock Mountain ridge and down to Fish Canyon (Trip 3) has entirely disappeared in the dense brush. ▲

3 Cienaga Public Campground to Pianobox, Fish Canyon Narrows, Rogers Camp, Lion Trail Camp

HIKE LENGTH:	12 miles round trip; 900' elevation gain
CLASSIFICATION:	Moderate
SEASON:	All year
TOPO MAPS:	Whitaker Peak, Liebre Mountain, Burnt Peak

Features

The long, shallow, meandering canyons in the northwest corner of Angeles National Forest are almost all laden with asphalt ribbon. One that is not, and is perhaps the most scenic of them all, is Fish Canyon, which runs south from Sawmill Mountain, then southwest into the Castaic Creek drainage.

Fish Canyon offers the best hiking in this part of the Angeles. An all-year stream descends its length, shaded most of the way by clusters of oak, sycamore, alder and willow. Most of the canyon is open and gentle-sloped—except for the ½ mile stretch of Fish Canyon Narrows, a slot through the mountain sometimes only a few yards wide. Abrupt, towering sidewalls of colorful rock make these narrows the most spectacular in the range—almost a Grand Canyon in miniature.

This very pleasant, almost level streamside trip ascends Fish Canyon from Cienaga Campground, follows a dirt road (closed to vehicles) to the Pianobox, an old mining prospect, passes through the scenic narrows to Rogers Trail Camp, and continues through the upper canyon to the delightful backcountry campsite of Lion Trail Camp. Be sure to wear stout and waterproof boots for the many stream crossings. You can rush through it in a day, or you can savor it on a two-day backpack outing, staying the night at either Rogers or Lion Camp.

Description

As of this writing (November 1999), the shorter western approach from Interstate 5 via Templin Highway, Castaic Creek and lower Fish Creek is indefinitely closed due to sever washouts. (Check with the Forest Service to learn if and when it might be reopened.)

The only present access is via the long, winding dirt road from Elizabeth Lake Canyon. From Castaic, drive northeast on the Elizabeth Lake Canyon Road (some signs say LAKE HUGHES ROAD) to its junction with the Warm Springs Canyon Road, 13 miles. Turn left (west) and follow the dirt road up over Warm Springs Divide and down to Cienaga Public Campground in Fish Canyon, 7 miles.

From just north of Cienaga Campground, walk north, up Fish Creek, on any of the several jeep tracks. In 200 yards they converge into one dirt road (closed to vehicles), which you follow to the Pianobox, 1 mile.

From the Pianobox your trail follows the canyon as it turns northeast, and you abruptly enter the narrows, cool and shady. Sheer sidewalls of reddish and yellowish rock make this area a favorite of shutter enthusiasts. Crossing and recrossing the stream, you work your way slowly upcanyon. In 2 miles you reach the oak- and sycamore-shaded bench of Rogers Camp, with stoves and tables. Just across the creek you can see a tunnel bored into solid rock, a relic of mining days. Beyond, the canyon rounds a bend, opens up, and resumes its northeast course. Your trail alternately follows the creek and climbs the slope to bypass narrows. Many sections of streamside trail are washed out, requiring much boulder-hopping and occasional bushwacking. In 6 miles you reach Lion Trail Camp, located on an oak-shaded bench at the confluence of Lion and Fish creeks. There are a stove, a fire-ring and a bench here at this most isolated of Angeles Forest trail camps, a great spot to savor true wilderness away from the crowds that infest so much of the Forest.

Return the same way. Or, you have an option.

You can continue up the Fish Canyon Trail, brushy in spots but passable, all the way to Atmore Meadows, 4½ miles (see Trip 2). A less strenuous option is to hike this trail downhill, from Atmore Meadows to the Pianobox, necessitating a rather long car shuttle.

The Burnt Peak Canyon Trail, shown on the Forest Service map, is, as of this writing, choked with brush and impassable.

The old trail from the Pianobox over the shoulder of Redrock Mountain to Redrock Canyon is no longer maintained by the Forest Service and is badly overgrown. So the once-popular 24-mile circle backpack trip up Fish Canyon and over the ridge to Bear Canyon, down Bear, Cienaga, and Redrock canyons is no longer an option. ▲

4 Bouquet Canyon to Big Oak Spring, Sierra Pelona

HIKE LENGTH:	7 miles round trip; 1300' elevation gain
CLASSIFICATION:	Moderate
SEASON:	All year
TOPO MAP:	Sleepy Valley

Features

The Sierra Pelona—bare-topped, wind-buffeted, lonely—forms a long arc across the northern mountains, separating Mint Canyon from first Bouquet Canyon and then Antelope Valley. Standing athwart the great wind funnel of Soledad Canyon, the crest is often battered by hurricane gusts. Sierra Pelona Lookout has recorded velocities of up to 100 miles per hour.

Nestled in protected recesses on the north slope of Sierra Pelona are isolated groves of live oak, some of them patriarchal in stature. According to the American Forestry Association's Big Tree Register, the world's largest recorded Canyon Live Oak—measuring 37 feet, 4 inches in trunk circumference—stands in a shallow draw on this north slope. Unfortunately, the tree was severely damaged in a brush fire many years ago. Today only its burned hulk remains, stark fingers pointing skyward.

This trip follows the Pacific Crest Trail up from Bouquet Canyon, visits Big Oak Spring and the charred remains of the world-record oak, and climbs to the top of Sierra Pelona for far-reaching vistas. Do it in summer, fall, winter or spring—but not on a windy day.

Description

From Antelope Valley Freeway (State Highway 14), turn west onto Palmdale Blvd., which becomes Elizabeth Lake Road. Follow it 9 miles, then turn left (south) on Bouquet Canyon Road, following it 5 miles to the Pacific Crest Trail crossing. Park in the clearing to your left (south).

Proceed up the signed PCT, climbing the north slope of chaparral-coated Sierra Pelona. As you gain altitude, you look down Bouquet Canyon, pastoral with its ranch houses and spreading oaks, with Bouquet Reservoir occasionally visible in the distance. You cross a poor jeep road and drop briefly into the upper reaches of Martindale Canyon before climbing again in a westward direction to a junction with the big Oak Spring trail, 2 miles from the start. Leave the PCT and follow the unimproved side trail through a grove of fire-damaged oaks.

In about 200 yards you round a point and see the remains of the champion oak up to your left. A distinct pathway climbs to Big Oak Spring, a trickle of water guarded by stinging nettles (painful if they penetrate the skin). Return to the junction and continue up the PCT, now climbing southward, to the bare crest of Sierra Pelona, 1 ½ more miles. Your vista now is impressive, especially if you walk a short distance west along the ridgetop fire road. Southeast, across the broad trench of Soledad Canyon, are the peaks of the main range—Mounts Gleason, Pacifico, Waterman and Williamson. Northwestward are the long hogbacks of Liebre and Sawmill Mountains. And north is the desert—sprawling, sun-bleached, seemingly endless.

An option is to walk 3 miles west along the ridgetop fire road to Mt. McDill (5187') for an even better view. Descend the way you came. If you don't mind bushwhacking, you can drop down the old Big Tree Trail, its upper end 50 yards east of the Big Oak Spring Trail, to Bouquet Canyon Road, then walk ½ mile east along the highway to your car. This trail has not been maintained in recent years. ▲

5 Placerita Canyon County Park to Walker Ranch Campground, Los Pinetos Spring, Los Pinetos Ridge, Firebreak Ridge, Manzanita Mountain

HIKE LENGTH:	8 miles round trip; 1800' elevation gain
CLASSIFICATION:	Moderate
SEASON:	October-June
TOPO MAPS:	Mint Canyon, San Fernando

Features

Gentle hills, rounded ridgetops, oak-dotted canyons, lots of chaparral—this describes the Placerita Canyon country near the western extremity of the main body of the San Gabriels. If you like your mountains simple, almost pastoral, much less abrupt than usual for the San Gabriels, this is a trip for you.

Placerita Canyon is etched in history. California's first gold rush occurred here in 1842, six years before John Marshall's famous discovery at Coloma. It began when Francisco Lopez of Rancho San Francisco (near present day Newhall) grew tired of chasing stray horses and sat down to rest under an oak tree. While resting, Lopez dug up a cluster of wild onions. Clinging to the roots were tiny gold nuggets. The discovery caused much excitement, and attracted miners from all over California. These San Fernando Placers, as they become known, produced several hundred thousand dollars in gold before the excitement died down a few years later.

Today the gold-rush area is preserved as Placerita Canyon County Park. The spot where Lopez is believed to have dug up the gold-bearing onions is known as "The Oak of the Golden Dream." It is marked with a plaque.

This trip goes up Placerita Canyon, shaded by overarching oaks and sycamores and graced with a trickling creek, to Walker Ranch Campground, then climbs through chaparral and oak to Los Pinetos Spring and on to the crest of Los Pinetos Ridge. Here you are rewarded with far-reaching vistas north across the peaceful Placerita and Sand Canyon country, and southward across sprawling San Fernando Valley. Then you descend via the new Firebreak Ridge-Manzanita Mountain Trail to complete a delightful loop hike.

Description

From the Antelope Valley Freeway (State Highway 14), turn right (east) onto Placerita Canyon Road and follow it to Placerita Canyon County Park, 2 miles. Park in the easternmost dirt parking area to your right, just before the Nature Center.

Cross the creek and pick up the Walker Ranch Trail, marked by a metal pole, which leads east, just to the right of the stream. Follow the trail as it winds its way up-canyon, crossing and recrossing the creek (water in spring, usually dry by midsummer), to Walker Ranch Group Campground, 2 miles. Walk east through the campground to a three-way trail junction. The trail left goes ⅓ mile to Placerita Canyon Road, an alternative trailhead. You turn right (south) and follow the marked Los Pinetos Trail as it climbs the chaparral- and oak-coated west slope of Los Pinetos Canyon to Los Pinetos Spring, nestled in a woodsy recess, 2 miles from Walker Campground. Here you meet a dirt road coming down from Los Pinetos Ridge fire road; don't take it. Just before the water tank, turn sharp right and follow the short-cut trail leading up to the ridgetop fire road, ½ mile.

If the day is hot, you may wish to return the way you came. There is no shade on the remainder of the loop trip. If the day is cool and you wish to continue, turn right (west) and follow the fire road uphill about ⅓ mile until you intersect the prominent firebreak leading north, down Firebreak Ridge. Turn right (north) and follow the firebreak as it descends north and then west, over several bumps, 2 miles to a junction with the trail leading right (north) down to Placerita Canyon County Park. (Note: You will see this trail to your right as you descend the last section of the firebreak; there is no sign at the junction, so watch for it carefully.) Descend the trail, passing a short side path left that leads 100 yards to the summit of Manzanita Mountain, to reach another junction just above the County Park. Go right, passing a water tank, and descend a final 200 feet to the Park. Cross Placerita Creek to your car. ▲

6 Dillon Divide to Pacoima Canyon, Dutch Louie Flat, Dagger Flat

HIKE LENGTH: 7 miles around trip; 800' elevation gain

CLASSIFICATION: Moderate

SEASON: October-May

TOPO MAP: Sunland

Features

Rugged Pacoima Creek cuts a deep swath from the west slopes of Mt. Gleason to the San Fernando Valley. An all-year stream rushes through the canyon bowels, shaded by oak, cottonwood, alder, and a handful of sycamores lower down. Dense chaparral clothes the north slope leading up to Santa Clara Divide, while the more protected south canyonside, below Mendenhall Ridge, is spotted with big-cone spruce.

"Pacoima" is derived from a Gabrielino Indian word, possibly meaning "running water." Indians once visited the lower canyon to gather scorns and hunt game. In more recent years, the canyon has been the scene of mining activities—gold, silver, titanium and graphite. Most notable were the G.C.K., or "Dutch Louie," placers, several thousand dollars in gold being recovered from the streambed. An old prospector known as Dutch Louie discovered the placers; to recover the gold, he and his associates diverted the stream by tunneling a temporary watercourse through a rock promontory. Today you can see the crumbling tunnel of this turn-of-the-century operation just upstream from Dutch Louie Flat. A half mile beyond, above Dagger Flat, are the remains of an old titanium mine.

This trip starts at Dillon Divide, drops down the dirt road into shady Pacoima Canyon to Dutch Louie Flat, and follows up the canyon, close by the sparkling creek, to Dagger Flat and beyond. Actually, you can make this walk as long as you want, by following up Pacoima Creek, under a cool canopy of live oak, alder, willow, and sycamore, as far as you wish to go.

Description

From the Foothill Freeway (State 210), just north of Hansen Dam, take the Osborne Street offramp. Follow Osborne Street north, with a short jog right at Foothill Blvd., into Little Tujunga Canyon. Osborne becomes Little Tujunga Road; follow it 7½ miles up to its intersection with gated Mendenhall Ridge Road at Dillon Divide. Park to the right (north) of the highway without blocking the fire road.

Pass the locked gate and follow dirt Mendenhall Ridge Road to a junction in ¼ mile; go left and follow the dirt road down into Pacoima Canyon to Dutch Louie Flat (formerly a campground), 2½ miles from Dillon Divide. Follow the old road upstream, crossing and recrossing the creek. In ¼ mile you round a bend and see, to your left, the remains of the old Dutch Louie tunnel. Just beyond, along the creek, is where placer gold was once recovered. About ½ mile beyond is Dagger Flat, where a turn-of-the-century prospector was allegedly stabbed to death. From here the old Dagger Flat Trail zigzags steeply up the north slope to Santa Clara Divide; don't take it—it's a shadeless bushwhack. You now have an option of lingering at Dagger Flat to check out the ghosts of the prospectors who once labored here for nature's elusive treasure, or continuing up beautiful Pacoima Creek as far as you want to go, first along an old dirt road, then on a streamside footpath that becomes indistinct at times.

Return the way you came.

(*Note*: The Angeles National Forest master plan calls for the building of a new trail from Dutch Louie Flat all the way up Pacoima Canyon to Mount Gleason. It probably will not become reality for a number of years. Check with the Tujunga Ranger District.) ▲

7   Gold Creek to Oak Spring, Fascination Spring

HIKE LENGTH:	8 miles round trip; 2000' elevation gain
CLASSIFICATION:	Moderate
SEASON:	November-May
TOPO MAP:	Sunland

Features

In the gentle hills above Little Tujunga Canyon are two delightful springs—little oak-sheltered eases nestled in hills covered with chaparral. Oak Spring lies in a shallow recess near the head of Oak Spring Canyon, just over the ridge from Gold Creek. Fascination Spring—one can only guess how it got this intriguing name—is hidden in a narrow crease on the south slope of the mountains, 2000' above the Sunland-Tujunga Valley.

You start from Gold Creek, Little Tujunga's major tributary. As the name suggests, Gold Creek was once the scene of feverish mining activity. Most storied were the so-called "Little Nugget" placers, gold being recovered right from the creekbed. The gold is gone now, and this is ranch country.

A good trail leads south from Gold Creek and climbs into the gentle hill country of Yerba Buena Ridge. A mile and a half up is Oak Spring, hidden in a small draw so that you don't see it until you're almost there. Then you climb over Yerba Buena Ridge and drop abruptly down to Fascination Spring. The two springs are shaded by oaks; the rest of the trip is through open chaparral. This is an ideal outing for a cool winter or spring day. Try it after a rain, when the springs bubble full and the aroma of damp chaparral perfumes the clean air.

Description

From Foothill Boulevard, right behind Hansen Flood Control Dam, drive 4¼ miles up Osborne Street, which becomes Little Tujunga Road. Turn right (east) onto Gold Creek Road and follow it 1 mile to the new Forest Service trailhead, ¼ mile before you reach the Brown Ranch gate. This new trail section eliminates the necessity of crossing private property. Park in the oak-shaded clearing adjacent to the trailhead.

Proceed via the new trail across Gold Creek and up the chaparral-coated south slope to a junction with the old trail, ¼ mile. Follow the old trail as it makes one long switchback, then climbs south up the chaparral-covered hillside. Vistas open up over the wrinkled Gold

Creek basin. The ranch you see down to the north is Paradise Ranch, scene of many a Cecil B. DeMille film extravaganza. Below to the east are the stone quarries where 770,000 tons of granite rock were removed for Hansen Dam in 1938-40. In 1¼ miles you cross a divide and drop down to lush Oak Spring—water except in the driest months. If it's a sunny day, the shade here is welcome. You'll see a fire road coming down to Oak Spring from the other side; don't take it. Walk down along the creek about 100 yards and pick up a trail that contours around the slope (south). This section of trail isn't as good as what you've just been over, but it's easily passable. Follow the trail through dense chaparral around the slope, across a small gully, and up to the Yerba Buena Ridge fire road, 1½ miles from Oak Spring. Here you have a spectacular panorama southward over the Tujunga and San Fernando valleys. Walk 100 yards down the road, then look for the trail dropping south down the steep mountainside. Fascination Spring is a mile down this trail (900' elevation loss), nestled in a small gully.

Return the same way, or you have two other options. Drop down the fire road below the spring, continuing south at a 4-way junction to Ebey Canyon and the maze of roads around the head of Oro Vista Avenue in Sunland, 2 miles. Or descend to the above-mentioned 4-way junction, then turn right(west) and follow the fire road 3½ miles to Little Tujunga Canyon. ▲

8   Big Tujunga to Gold Canyon, Yerba Buena Ridge

HIKE LENGTH: 6 miles round trip; 1600' elevation gain
CLASSIFICATION: Moderate
SEASON: November-May
TOPO MAP: Sunland

Features

Gold Canyon is almost unknown to hikers and seldom visited. Nevertheless, the canyon retains spots of its old charms, and it offers the hiker more solitude than its over-used, over-the-ridge neighbor Trail Canyon (see Trip 9). According to geologists, the Sierra Madre Fault runs right through the canyon, and evidences of past geologic activity are found in the twisted, whitish cliffs at the canyon's head. As implied by its name, Gold Canyon was the scene of prospecting activities in past years. Apparently not much gold was found here, as no patented claims were ever recorded.

An old pack trail, once used by miners traveling between Big and Little Tujunga, ascends the canyon to Yerba Buena Ridge, where it meets a fire road. The footpath is no longer maintained by the Forest Service, but it is passable although partially washed out along the streambed. Chances are you'll have the canyon to yourself; most hikers prefer better-known Trail Canyon.

Description

From Foothill Boulevard in Sunland, drive 3½ miles up Mount Gleason Avenue, which turns into Big Tujunga Canyon Road, to a spot 1 mile beyond County Detention Camp #15, about 300 yards before the Angeles National Forest entry sign. (If you cross the main highway bridge, you've driven 1 mile too far.) Park off the highway.

Ford Big Tujunga Creek to the west side (easy boulderhop in low water; dangerous in high water—if water high, drive on up the highway across the bridge and then work your way down-canyon on the west bank under the bridge). Proceed up-canyon to the narrow mouth of Gold Canyon, ½ mile. Turn west up Gold Canyon and pick up the trail that follows the canyon bottom, mostly along a low bench on the left bank, through a cluster of alders and oaks. Much of the trail along the creek is washed out, and you must boulder-hop, but the boulders are small and it's not difficult. The trail—what's left of it—follows Gold Creek for about 1¼ miles, then starts switchbacking up the left (southwest) slope. The spot where it leaves the canyon is easy to miss; look for it in a cluster of oaks and several spruces to the left of the stream.

Ceanothus in bloom above Big Tujunga Canyon

This upward trail has not been worked in recent years and is badly overgrown in places. You zigzag up through chaparral, negotiating some eroded spots near the top, to the Yerba Buena Ridge fire road in 1½ miles. As you rise out of the canyon, vistas open up. You look straight down Gold Creek to Big Tujunga, which continues in the same beeline—evidence of the Sierra Madre Fault. On the distant skyline are Josephine, Strawberry and Disappointment peaks. Farther up the trail, you get a close-up look at the strange whitish cliffs—twisted and folded—further evidence of earth forces at work along the faultline. From Yerba Buena Ridge, you get a superb view westward into the more gentle Gold Creek-Little Tujunga country.

Return the same way. An option is to follow the Yerba Buena Ridge fire road north to Gold Canyon Saddle, northeast to Gold Creek Saddle, and southeast down the ridge to the Upper Trail Canyon Road and Big Tujunga—a long, round-about walk, 8 miles total. This requires a 2-mile car shuttle from Gold Creek to Trail Canyon. ▲

9   Big Tujunga to Tom Lucas Trail Camp, Big Cienaga

HIKE LENGTH:	8 miles round trip; 2000' elevation gain
CLASSIFICATION:	Moderate
SEASON:	November-June
TOPO MAPS:	Sunland, Condor Peak

Features

Trail Canyon cuts a deep swath through the western front country of the San Gabriels. Steep, chaparral-blanketed ridges enclose it on both sides, and the great arched head of Condor Peak looms high on the eastern skyline. The canyon was once a lush and verdant oasis, until the 1975 Big Tujunga fire blackened the steep slopes and burned away much of the streamside greenery. Still, there are a number of delightful wooded haunts scattered here and there in the canyon, making the hike well worth the effort. The scenic highlight is Trail Canyon Falls, two miles up-canyon, a delicate ribbon of whitewater swishing 30 feet into a cool sanctuary of alders and ferns.

It is appropriate that the campground be named after Tom Lucas, one of the real pioneers of the Big Tujunga. "Barefoot Tom," as he was known to his mountain friends, was one of the first forest rangers in the old San Gabriel Timberland Reserve, a grizzly bear hunter, and in his later years a rancher at the old Ybarra Ranch in the Big Tujunga. He knew the mountain country as few others did.

Description

From Foothill Boulevard in Sunland, drive 5 miles up Mount Gleason Avenue, which turns into Big Tujunga Canyon Road, to Upper Trail Canyon Road, marked by a wooden sign. Turn left and drive up the winding dirt road to a junction, then go right and down into Trail Canyon to a parking area beneath live oaks.

Walk past the locked gate and follow the dirt road, passing some private cabins and crossing the creek on some well-placed planks. The old road climbs the east slope, then drops steeply back into the canyon and ends. Ford the creek and pick up the trail as it threads its way up the boulder-filled canyon, crossing and re crossing the creek in foot-wetting fords. In 1 mile you reach a large, open bench on the left (west) side of the creek. Here your trail leaves the creekside and switchbacks steeply up to the left, then climbs steadily up the slope to get around Trail Canyon Falls. In another ½ mile you round a sharp turn and then another turn, where the falls come into view, impressive as they plunge into the canyon depths below you. Just beyond where the trail again turns north, you will notice a narrow sidepath through the brush on which hikers have descended to the falls—very steep and loose footing. Continuing on the main trail, you drop back into the canyon above the falls and ford the creek again. Over the next 2 miles you follow the creek up-canyon, fording the stream several times, making your way around and through boulder fields, and reaches old Tom Lucas campsite, no longer maintained by the Forest Service. There is a rock fire-ring here, and several small flats for sleeping. A mile beyond, where the canyon bends northward, your trail switchbacks up the slope, reapproaches the creek, crosses it, and reaches new Tom Lucas Trail Camp, with picnic tables and cleared camping areas amid alders and oaks, 4 miles from the start. This lush area at the head of Trail Canyon Creek is known as Big Cienaga.

From new Tom Lucas, the trail climbs, with several long switchbacks, to a branch of the Mendenhall Ridge fire road (see Trip 10), but you turn back at Big Cienaga.

As always, as you stroll down-canyon on the return trip, new vistas open up and you get a different perspective of the country. Most impressive, as you get back into the lower canyon, is the great buttress of Mt. Lukens, towering on the southern skyline. This front-range country may be tamed and overrun by man, but it retains its rugged appeal. If it's late afternoon, chances are that a purplish haze will be adding a mystical quality to the mountain landscape. Mt. Lukens may be a shadowy ghost in the distance.

A scenic option, 14 miles altogether, is to follow the Trail Canyon Trail up to its end at the spur road southeast of Iron Mountain, follow the spur road to the main Mendenhall fire road, turn left (west) and follow the latter 3 miles to the Yerba Buena Trail (marked by a wooden sign as of Dec. 1984), descend the trail to Gold Creek Saddle, 2 miles, then descend the Gold Canyon fire road to Upper Trail Canyon road and follow the latter down to your car. ▲

10 Big Tujunga to Tom Lucas Trail Camp, Indian Ben Saddle, Upper Pacoima Canyon, Deer Spring, Messenger Flats Campground

HIKE LENGTH: 11 miles one way; 4200' elevation gain

CLASSIFICATION: Strenuous (one day); Moderate (two days)

SEASON: May-October

TOPO MAPS: Sunland, Condor Peak, Acton

Features

This delightful one-way trip (a car shuttle is recommended) climbs all the way up Trail Canyon to Mendenhall Ridge, then ascends Upper Pacoima Canyon to Deer Springs and pine-shaded Messenger Flats Campground just below Mt. Gleason. You get superb views over the chaparral-clad and pine-dotted high country at the west end of the San Gabriels. You should be particularly delighted with the new trail stretch in Upper Pacoima, a canyon oasis of big-cone spruce and ponderosa and sugar pine seldom trod by hikers.

This trip is best done as an overnight backpack, camping at Tom Lucas Trail Camp a third of the way up. You can do it in one long day, if you're a glutton for punishment. Unless you want to return the same long way and double your mileage, have someone meet you at Messenger Flats Campground, a 12-mile drive up Mt. Gleason Road from Mill Creek Summit on the Angeles Forest Highway. Bring a canteen; there is all-year water in Trail Canyon and Upper Pacoima, but none in the open 3-mile stretch over Mendenhall Ridge and Indian Ben Saddle. Better check with the Forest Service before you make the trip: 6100' Messenger Flats Campground is sometimes closed by snow as late as mid-May, and lower Trail Canyon may be closed as a fire hazard on hot summer days.

Description

Driving directions for the start of the trip are the same as for Trip 9. For Messenger Flats Campground, where you should he picked up, drive up the Angeles Crest Highway to Clear Creek Junction, then left up the Angeles Forest Highway (L.A. County Road N3) to Mill Creek Summit, 23 miles from La Canada. Turn left (west) onto Mt. Gleason Road and follow it 12 miles to the campground.

Walk 3½ miles up Trail Canyon to Tom Lucas Trail Camp (see Trip 9 for trail description). Fill your canteen here. Continue up the trail through the marshy stretch known as Big Cienaga. Just beyond, your trail leaves the tree-shaded canyon and climbs up chaparral-blanketed slopes, passing a junction with the Condor Peak Trail, to a ridgetop where it meets a spur of the Mendenhall Ridge fire road. Follow the spur road, then the main fire road to Indian Ben Saddle (named for a gold prospector during depression days). Here you pick up the new Upper Pacoima Trail leading northeast into the canyon. Follow the trail as it contours, then drops to the forested bottom of Pacoima Canyon and follows the creek some 2 miles before switchbacking up to Deer Spring. Go left at a trail junction there and follow the new path 1 mile to Messenger Flats Campground. (The trail to the right at Deer Springs goes ½ mile up to Lightning Point Group Campground; camping here is by reservation only.) ▲

11 Big Tujunga to Mt. Lukens via Stone Canyon Trail

HIKE LENGTH:	8 miles round trip; 3200′ elevation gain
CLASSIFICATION:	Moderate
SEASON:	November-May
TOPO MAP:	Condor Peak

Features

Mt. Lukens, a massive hogback mountain, lies just within the boundaries of Los Angeles, making it the highest point in the city. Years ago it was known as "Sister Elsie Peak" to commemorate the good deeds of a Roman Catholic nun in the La Crescenta Valley. Sister Elsie, in charge of *El Rancho de Dos Hermanas* orphanage for Indian children, was much loved for her kind acts, particularly for nursing victims of a smallpox epidemic, during which she is reported to have lost her life. In the 1920s the Forest Service renamed the peak "Mt. Lukens" in honor of Theodore P. Lukens, one-time Angeles National Forest Supervisor, famed for his reforestation efforts at Henninger Flat. A fire lookout was built on the summit in 1923; in 1937 it was moved to nearby Josephine Peak because, even then, urban haze was interfering with observation. The 1975 Big Tujunga holocaust seared the slopes of the mountain, and it will be several years before the chaparral is rich and green again.

This trip is the best and shortest way to climb Mt. Lukens—the only way that is not via a long, monotonous fire road. But it is exceptionally steep. The old Stone Canyon Trail—not regularly maintained but readily passable—wastes no mileage in going from Big Tujunga to the summit; it proceeds right up the north slope, without a level stretch until you reach the summit ridge. You're on burned slopes most of the way, with an occasional big-cone spruce or two for welcome shade. Carry a canteen; you pass a sluggish spring about half way up, but the water is not dependable.

Description

From Foothill Boulevard in Sunland, drive 6 miles up Mount Gleason Avenue, which becomes Big Tujunga Canyon Road, to its intersection with Doske Road. Turn right and descend Doske Road to Stonyvale Road along the canyon bottom. Turn left (upstream) on Stonyvale Road and drive about ½ mile. The trailhead is marked with a black steel pipe with the words "Stone Canyon Trail" painted on it, to

Sunset over Mt. Lukens

Huntington Library

your right. Park off the shoulder of the road opposite where you see the trail.

Cross the Big Tujunga—difficult if not impossible when the water is high—and head toward the trail on a sloping bench left (east) of Stone Canyon Creek. Once you locate the trail, there's no problem. Follow it as it zigzags steeply up the ridge left of Stone Canyon. In about 2 miles you pass a small spring—a trickle of water during rainy season. In 3½ miles you reach an old fire road on the ridge northwest of the summit. Turn left (southeast) and follow the bare path ¼ mile to the top.

After enjoying the spectacular vista of the front-range country and the city (if the smog isn't too bad), return the way you came. Or, you can continue southeast and descend the long fire road and Dark Canyon Trail to the Angeles Crest Highway (see Trip 13). This latter option requires a car shuttle. ▲

12 Big Tujunga to Condor Peak via Fox Divide

HIKE LENGTH: 16 miles round trip; 3400' elevation gain
CLASSIFICATION: Strenuous
SEASON: November-May
TOPO MAP: Condor Peak

Features

There are no condors on Condor Peak, nor anywhere else in the San Gabriels today. The last redoubt of these magnificent birds is in the Sespe Creek area of Los Padres National Forest, some fifty miles northwest. Years ago, before humans disturbed its fragile habitat, this fast-vanishing species was common in all the Southern California mountains. According to mountain pioneer Faust Havermale, Condor Peak was so named because these monarchs of the air once nested here. Havermale wrote that he personally sighted 12 of these giant birds soaring around the peak, back around the turn of the century.

But nostalgia for the departed birds is not the only reason for climbing Condor Peak. From its airy summit, you get a breathtaking panorama over the rugged Big Tujunga country and beyond to the major peaks of the front range—Lukens to the south; Josephine, Strawberry and San Gabriel to the southeast. The mile-high atmosphere is fresh and clean and invigorating.

As along all the trails out of Big Tujunga, the 1975 holocaust destroyed most of the ground cover and it will be a number of years before the chaparral again looms tall and green. There is no shade on the entire route, so the trip should be done on a cool winter or spring day. Carry two canteens; the one water source enroute is not always flowing.

Description

You have a choice of two trailheads for this trip.

From Foothill Boulevard in Sunland, drive up Mount Gleason Avenue, which turns into Big Tujunga Canyon Road. In 7¼ miles you reach a parking area opposite the Vogel Flat Road intersection, where the old trail begins. 1½ miles farther on Big Tujunga Canyon Road is the new trailhead, across from the Grizzly Flat Plantation sign and parking area. Both trailheads are unsigned.

For the old trail from Vogel Flat (recommended by this writer), walk about 150 yards up the highway to a small culvert on the left side of the road. Pick up the trail where it enters the chaparral, then bear right up the slope, cross a low bridge, and drop, then contour and finally climb around a small canyon just above the highway. If you wish to walk the new trail that begins 1½ miles farther up the road, cross the highway from the Grizzly Flat clearing and walk about 30 yards back; you will easily locate it winding up the brush-covered slope. (This new trail is longer and descends almost a mile to meet the old trail, which means you must climb back up to the highway on your return trip; therefore, the old trail is the better route.)

The two trails intersect in a mile. For 3 more miles, the now-single trail zigzags up the divide between Vogel and Fusier canyons, traverses a slope, passes a small creek (usually water in springtime), and finally reaches the high ridge between the head of Vogel Canyon and Fox Creek. You climb steeply, then contour around the west side of Fox Peak before ascending the ridgetop firebreak over three false summits to the true summit of Condor Peak (5439′).

Descend by the same route. Or, with a 3-mile car shuttle, you can drop down the north slope of Condor Peak and follow the new trail north to its intersection with the Trail Canyon Trail, then descend the latter to Big Tujunga (see Trip 9). You can also use this route to climb the peak. ▲

13   Angeles Crest Highway to Grizzly Flat and Vasquez Creek

HIKE LENGTH: 4.5 miles round trip; 1100' elevation gain

CLASSIFICATION: Easy

SEASON: November-May

TOPO MAP: Condor Peak

Features

Grizzly Flat is a rather conspicuous sloping bench on the mountainside south of Big Tujunga, directly above where the great canyon elbows northeast. The flat is cut abruptly on both sides—on the west by an unnamed gully, on the east by spruce-shaded Vasquez Creek. There was once a healthy forest here, but fire burned most of it away in 1959. The flat is now grass-covered, and the trees are starting to grow back, but very slowly. What humans destroy in a careless instant, nature takes years to rebuild.

Grizzly Flat, Vasquez Creek—these names bring to mind two scourges of the San Gabriels of yesteryear: grizzly bears and *bandidos*.

Grizzlies once abounded in these mountains, and oldtimers' recollections are full of exciting encounters with these forest behemoths, which seemed to favor the Big Tujunga region particularly. The last verified grizzly bear south of the Tehachapis was killed in lower Big Tujunga in 1916.

Vasquez Creek immortalizes an 1874 foray by Southern California's most famous bandit, Tiburcio Vasquez. After raiding the Repetto Ranch, in the hills south of San Gabriel Valley, Vasquez and his small gang took off with $500, hotly pursued by a sheriff's posse. The outlaws hurried up the Arroyo Seco, ascended Dark Canyon to the divide, and dropped down an unnamed creek into Big Tujunga. The posse, guessing that Vasquez was heading for Big Tujunga, backtracked and raced around to the canyon entrance to block his escape. But the *bandidos*, urging their horses to the limit, just managed to race out of the canyon ahead of the converging lawmen. Since this episode, the stream in the gully down which the bandits descended to Big Tujunga has been known as Vasquez Creek.

Today this mountainside is serene, away from the more frequented parts of the front range. You use the upper part of the historic Dark Canyon Trail, recently cleared by volunteers, then descend a fire road to Grizzly Flat and its tree plantation. A short stretch of easy cross-country walking gets you to Vasquez Creek.

Description

Drive up the Angeles Crest Highway 6.1 miles from La Canada to a small parking area (big enough for four or five cars) opposite highway mileage marker 30.02.

The trail begins at the lower (south) end of the parking area and climbs steeply up the slope to a loop road at the lower edge of a tree plantation, ½ mile. Go right and follow the dirt road up to fire road 2N80 on the crest of the divide between the Arroyo Seco and Big Tujunga watersheds. Cross 2N80 and descend an unmarked dirt road to Grizzly Flat, amid a grove of pines planted by the Forest Service after a fire in 1958. A faint, unmarked trail goes right (northeast) to Vasquez Creek, ¼ mile. There is no trail along Vasquez Creek, but you can follow the creek a short distance in either direction.

With a car shuttle, you can follow the trail northwest from Grizzly Flat, crossing a small unnamed creek, down to Big Tujunga Creek, which you must ford, and on to Stonyvale Picnic Area, 3 miles. See Trip 11 for driving route (Stonyvale Picnic Area is just beyond the Stone Canyon trailhead). Avoid this alternative after heavy rains; Big Tujunga swells to a raging torrent. ▲

14   Tujunga to Mt. Lukens via Haines Canyon Trail

HIKE LENGTH:	8 miles round trip; 2800' elevation gain
CLASSIFICATION:	Moderate
SEASON:	November-May
TOPO MAP:	Condor Peak

Features

This is the old Sister Elsie Trail up the southwest shoulder of Mt. Lukens, reworked in recent years by Sierra Club volunteers. There is little shade enroute—thanks to the 1975 Big Tujunga holocaust—so do it on a cool winter or spring day.

Description

From Foothill Blvd. in Tujunga, go north on Haines Canyon Ave., jogging ½ block east at Day St. Continue up Haines Canyon Road to the locked gate just short of the debris dam. Park here.

Walk up the road beyond the gate. One fourth mile beyond the debris dam the main road turns right and climbs the south canyon slope. Go left here 200 yards on a poor dirt road, passing a cement water tank. In ½ mile the road becomes a trail. About ¼ mile farther you reach a junction—just short of a stream crossing. Continue straight ahead, crossing the creek. (The trail to the right switchbacks up the canyon wall and joins the fire road halfway to the summit.) Your trail becomes increasingly indistinct as you follow the canyon bottom ½ mile, then turn right and zigzag up a steep side canyon. Here you are in oak woodland—one of the few areas on the mountain untouched by the 1975 fire. In ½ mile, near the canyon head, your trail abruptly zigs left and reaches a saddle on Mt. Lukens' east ridge, where views open northward across the mighty gorge of Big Tujunga. You climb along the ridgetop ¼ mile, then contour left along the steep north slope of the ridge to a junction with the Stone Canyon Trail (see Trip 11). Follow the latter, then the fireroad to the summit. ▲

15 Altadena to Oakwilde via Arroyo Seco

HIKE LENGTH:	9 miles round trip; 900' elevation gain
CLASSIFICATION:	Moderate
SEASON:	November-May
TOPO MAP:	Pasadena

Features

The Arroyo Seco today is largely bypassed and forgotten. Fifty years ago it was one of the most popular vacation spots in the range. Under its luxuriant cover of willow, sycamore, alder and bay, the canyon reverberated with the lusty shouts and merry songs of hikers and campers. The lower reaches were dotted with rustic cabins and well-used picnic spots. This was before the Angeles Crest Highway provided ready access into the mountains, climbing high on the west slope of the canyon. Now nature's stillness reigns supreme in the canyon, broken only by the gentle murmur of stream, the soft rustle of sycamore leaves, and—as a reminder of civilization's nearness—the occasional muffled roar of an automobile rounding a curve far above.

About halfway up this great gorge, on a forested streamside bench, is Oakwilde Picnic Area—tables and stoves. Here, in 1911, J. R. Phillips fashioned a tourist resort—old Camp Oak Wilde. For almost three decades, until it was nearly obliterated in the 1938 flood, this was a favorite spot of vacationing Southlanders. In the 1920s a road was built up the lower Arroyo Seco to the camp; it too was severely damaged in the greatest torrent ever known in the San Gabriels. Today, only remnants of the road remain, and a few stone foundations at Oakwilde are the only signs of what once went on here.

Time and nature's gradual healing process have restored much of the beauty of the lower Arroyo Seco, although parts of it have been permanently marred by man's work—most notably the Brown Canyon Debris Dam. Still, there is much to be seen and enjoyed in this great canyon; this trail trip gives you a fair sampling.

Description

From 210 Freeway, take the Arroyo Blvd. offramp and drive north on Arroyo, which promptly becomes Windsor Avenue. Continue north ¾ mile to the intersection with Ventura Street.

You will notice two roads—both with gates usually locked—leading north down toward the canyon entrance. Take the right (eastern) of the two; the left road goes to the JPL parking lot. Proceed on foot down the road, which gains the Arroyo Seco entrance in ½ mile. You pass the assorted markings of the Pasadena Water Department—fences, retaining walls, gaging stations, and a host of warning signs—and reach Forest Service residences in another ½ mile. Go left at a road fork, as indicated by the GABRIELINO TRAIL sign. Now the canyon closes in and the scenery becomes more woodsy—giant canyon oaks, alders, willows, sycamores, even a few eucalyptus trees from resort days. This is both a hiking and an equestrian route, so you'll most likely pass horseback riders. The trail alternates between following the old road and stream-hopping where roadbed and bridges have washed out.

A half mile above the Forest Service residences is Teddy's Outpost Picnic Area—named for a small roadside resort operated by Theodore "Teddy" Syvertson from 1914 to 1915. In another ½ mile you reach the Gould Mesa Campground, honoring Will Gould, who homesteaded here in the '90s, and just beyond, a sideroad leading up to Gould Mesa and the Angeles Crest Highway. Nine Picnic Area is ⅓ mile farther. Above Nine the canyon narrows, twists and turns, and remnants of the old road become less evident. In another ¾ mile you reach Paul Little Memorial Picnic Area, 100 feet to your left. Going right, the trail climbs up the steep east slope of the canyon to get around Brown Canyon Debris Dam, then drops back into the gorge and rounds two sharp bends before reaching Oakwilde, 4½ miles from the start. Here, amid the crumbling foundations of the old road's-end resort, under live oaks and alders, the Forest Service has built Oakwilde Trail Camp, with tables and stoves.

Return the way you came. ▲

16 Angeles Crest Highway to Oakwilde, Arroyo Seco, Switzer Trail Camp, and Switzer Picnic Area

HIKE LENGTH:	10½ miles round trip; 1500' elevation gain
CLASSIFICATION:	Moderate
SEASON:	November-May
TOPO MAPS:	Condor Peak, Pasadena

Features

This trip drops into the Arroyo Seco from high on the Angeles Crest Highway, then traverses the wild central portion of the Arroyo Seco Trail to Switzer Campground. Enroute it passes through the sites of two once-famous mountain resorts-Oak Wilde and Switzer's Camp. To avoid the difficult middle gorge of the Arroyo Seco, known as "Royal Gorge" to old-timers, the trail climbs up and over chaparral-blanketed ridges, not very pleasant walking on a hot day. Do it when the weather is cool. A car shuttle is required.

Description

The historic Dark Canyon Trail is temporarily impassable because of a massive slide. Until the trail is rebuilt by the Forest Service, hikers must use the paved fire road down into the Arroyo Seco from Gould Mesa. Drive from La Canada up the Angeles Crest Highway 2 miles,

Switzer's Chapel (1924-1959)

Huntington Library

just past the first big bend, to a gated road on your right, under a powerline, where a small wooden sign points right (east) and indicates GABRIELINO TRAIL. Park in the clearing on your right just below the gated road.

Proceed around the locked gate through a hikers' entrance to the right, then follow the road east, passing a power substation on your right. Beyond the station, the road narrows and winds steeply down into the Arroyo Seco, where you intersect the Arroyo Seco Trail, ½ mile. Follow the trail upstream, crossing and recrossing the creek, climbing the east slope to pass the Brown Canyon Dam, and then dropping back to the canyon floor and fording the creek once again to the Oakwilde Picnic Area, 3½ miles from the start. Continue up the Arroyo Seco, fording and refording the stream (footwetting in times of high water). About a mile above Oakwilde the arroyo makes a sharp turn east and becomes a narrow gorge, difficult of passage. Here the trail leaves the main canyon, ascends the east fork of Long Canyon, and climbs high over chaparral ridges before dropping back into the Arroyo Seco at Switzer's Trail Camp, 3½ miles from Oakwilde. Here, shaded by magnificent alders and oaks, once stood the most popular trail resort in the range (see Trip 17). Today the buildings are gone. A mile farther up canyon, partly by boulder-hopping and partly on the remains of an old road, you reach spacious Switzer Picnic Area, and a paved road up to the Angeles Crest Highway.

As an alternative you can do this trip in reverse, starting at Switzer Picnic Area and finishing on Gould Mesa—mostly downhill, with a 500' gain at the end. ▲

17 Switzer Picnic Area to Commodore Switzer Trail Camp, Switzer Falls, Arroyo Seco Cascades

HIKE LENGTH:	4 miles round trip; 600' elevation loss and gain
CLASSIFICATION:	Easy
SEASON:	November-June
TOPO MAP:	Condor Peak

Features

Once the name Switzer was almost synonymous with Arroyo Seco. This was when Switzer's Camp was the most famous trail resort in the range. By foot, by horse, or by burro-back hundreds of people traveled up the Arroyo Seco every weekend to visit this picturesque, woodsy hostelry above Switzer Falls.

It was Commodore Perry Switzer, along with the mountain-loving Watermans—Bob and Lit—who fashioned this wilderness resort back in 1884. Twice weekly, Switzer led his burro train up the tortuous Arroyo Seco Trail—sixty stream crossings and endless switchbacks. A cowhorn was left dangling on a manzanita bush ½ mile below camp, with printed instructions to issue forth a blast for each hungry guest. When the tired visitors finally reached camp, they would find a sizzling dinner awaiting them. Trout from the adjacent stream were featured.

It was under hospitable Lloyd and Bertha Austin (1912-1936) that Switzer's really became the Number One resort in the range. The warmth and friendliness of the Austins attracted thousands from all walks of life. Among those who signed the guest register were Henry Ford, Shirley Temple, Clark Gable, and Mary Pickford. LEAVE YOUR CARES AND ANIMALS THIS SIDE OF THE STREAM was the sign that greeted approaching visitors; another sign over the lodge door read THE AUSTIN HOME ...AND YOURS. So that his guests would have the opportunity for a variety of experiences, Austin added a tennis court, a croquet court, a well-stocked library, a children's playground, an open-air dance floor for "Switzer Saturday Nights," and a miniature Christ Chapel perched above the falls for Sunday morning worship.

All this is gone now, the victim of progress in the form of the Angeles Crest Highway. With people able to drive in minutes to places that once required hours or days of strenuous hiking, the old camp lost its wilderness appeal. After withering for two decades, it was finally abandoned and all buildings removed in 1959. Today the sylvan bench just above the falls is occupied by Commodore Switzer Trail Camp—a wilderness campsite with no facilities.

This trip is a delightful streamside stroll under alder, oak, maple and spruce. You visit the old campsite and then descend into the narrow "Royal Gorge" of the Arroyo Seco for a close-up view of plunging Switzer Falls and the numerous little pools and cascades that dot the shady chasm. (Don't try to climb the falls; several have been injured in the attempt.)

Description

Drive up the Angeles Crest Highway 10½ miles from La Canada to the side road down to Switzer Picnic Area, ½ mile past the junction of the Angeles Crest and Angeles Forest highways. Turn right and descend to the parking area outside the picnic area, ¼ mile.

Cross the bridge and follow the trail down-canyon. It is a mile to Commodore Switzer Trail Camp; part of the distance you must boulder-hop, where the trail is washed out. From the trail camp, cross the stream and follow the trail as it climbs and then contours along the west slope above the falls. *Do not* follow the creek below camp; it abruptly drops fifty feet at the falls. About ¼ mile beyond camp is an unmarked junction: the right (southwest) fork is the main Arroyo Seco Trail, down to Oakwilde and Pasadena (see Trips 15 and 16). Go left (southeast), dropping into the gorge of the Arroyo Seco below the falls. When you reach the creek, turn upstream ¼ mile to Switzer Falls. Remember, don't climb the sheer rock sidewalls of the falls. Then turn back downstream and follow the woodsy gorge past numerous sparkling pools and miniature cascades, about a mile to the Bear Canyon junction. This secluded part of the Arroyo Seco is one of the most beautiful spots in the front range, beckoning to any who are willing to leave their automobile and stroll for a leisurely two or three hours.

Return the way you came. ▲

18 Switzer Picnic Area to Commodore Switzer Trail Camp, Bear Canyon, Bear Canyon Trail Camp

HIKE LENGTH: 8 miles round trip; 1000' elevation gain

CLASSIFICATION: Moderate

SEASON: November-June

TOPO MAPS: Condor Peak, Pasadena

Features

Rugged Bear Canyon, the largest tributary of the Arroyo Seco, is as near to being wilderness as any place in the front range of the San Gabriels. A beautiful stream, with mirror-like pools, cascades, and small waterfalls, graces the canyon bottom. Stately big-cone spruces keep much of the creek in near-perpetual shade. By a fortunate accident of geography, Bear Canyon is isolated from man's frenetic activity even though it lies smack in the middle of the much-abused front range. Although highways and fire roads virtually circle the chasm, none comes quite close enough to violate its sanctity.

This trip descends the Arroyo Seco to its junction with Bear Canyon, then ascends the latter to lonely Bear Canyon Trail Camp, set on a spruce-shaded streamside bench about halfway up the canyon. You

Arroyo Seco above Switzer Trail Camp

will be tempted to stay the night here, where nature retains a small foothold, and civilization—just over the ridge—seems far away.

Wear lug-soled boots; the old Tom Sloan Trail that once traveled the length of the canyon is in poor shape, and you must scramble and boulder-hop much of the way.

Description

Drive up the Angeles Crest Highway 10½ miles from La Canada to the side road down to Switzer Picnic Area, ½ mile past the junction of the Angeles Crest and Angeles Forest highways. Turn right and descend to the parking area outside the campground, ¼ mile.

Cross the bridge and follow the trail down-canyon, past Commodore Switzer Trail Camp, and down into the gorge of the

Arroyo Seco below Switzer Falls (see Trip 17 for details). Continue down the Arroyo Seco gorge another ¾ mile to the junction with Bear Canyon (2 miles from the start). The trail turns east up Bear Canyon, skipping from side to side. Frequently it disappears; continue along the creek and you will find it again. About 2 miles up the canyon, the trail climbs onto a forested bench on the south slope, about 20' above the stream. Here is Bear Canyon Trail Camp. Be on the lookout for this spot; it is easy to miss the trail leading up the slope.

This trip returns the same way. You also have the option of continuing up the canyon trail another 2 miles, then steeply up to Tom Sloan Saddle and the Mt. Lowe fire road (see Trip 33), or dropping from the saddle into Millard Canyon (see Trip 19). Either of these options requires a car shuttle. ▲

19 Millard Canyon to Dawn Mine

HIKE LENGTH:	5 miles round trip; 1200' elevation gain
CLASSIFICATION:	Moderate
SEASON:	November-May
TOPO MAP:	Pasadena

Features

Woodsy Millard Canyon ranks as one of the more pleasant retreats in the front range of the San Gabriels. Nestled deep between Sunset Ridge and Brown Mountain, the canyon seldom suffers the full glare of sunlight. Beneath overarching oaks and sycamores, the small stream glides and dances over water-tempered boulders, finally to tumble headlong over Millard Falls.

Deep in the upper reaches of Millard Canyon are the remains of the Dawn Mine, the most storied gold prospect in the front range. Gold was discovered here in 1895, and the ore-bearing veins were worked on and off with varying degrees of success into the early 1950s. No great amount of gold was ever recovered, despite repeated boasts of imminent bonanzas by overoptimistic prospectors.

The trail up Millard Canyon to Dawn Mine is no longer maintained. In its middle and upper stretches, where it closely parallels the stream, it is almost gone, and boulderhopping is the order of the day. But the canyon is a sylvan delight, where you can temporarily forget your proximity to civilization. It is a peaceful place to while away the hours, to saunter rather than stride.

Description

From Loma Alta Drive in Altadena, turn north on Chaney Trail Drive and follow it to the junction atop Sunset Ridge; turn right and park outside the locked gate blocking the Sunset Ridge fire road.

Hike up the Sunset Ridge fire road about 400 yards to a distinct but unmarked trail leading left, around the ridge and down into Millard Canyon above the falls. Just before you reach the canyon bottom, at a trail junction, go left (the right branch leads back up to Sunset Ridge fire road). When the trail reaches the streambed it all but disappears in a jumble of boulders. As you scramble up-stream, you will meet stretches of the old trail here and there, but mostly you will boulder-hop. After slightly more than a mile, the canyon suddenly elbows north; just beyond you must climb steeply up the right (east) bank to circumvent a rocky obstruction. Less than a mile of additional boulderhopping brings you to the woodsy haunt where once was Dawn Mine. Not much remains—scattered diggings and pieces of rusted mill machinery, and a boarded-up tunnel. Do not try to explore the tunnel; there are water-filled holes difficult to detect. Leading in from the right (east) is the Dawn Mine Trail, via which burros once carried ore from the mine to the Mount Lowe Railway, recently put back in good condition by the JPL Hiking Club.

But this particular trail trip ends at Dawn Mine, so after looking over the shaded sanctuary, return the way you came. ▲

Dawn Mine tunnel

20 Millard Canyon to Millard Canyon Falls

HIKE LENGTH:	1 mile round trip; 150' elevation gain
CLASSIFICATION:	Easy
SEASON:	November-May
TOPO MAP:	Pasadena

Features

Of the two dozen or so real waterfalls in the San Gabriel Mountains, only four are readily accessible to the leisurely stroller. Millard Canyon Falls is one of these. The 50' falls are wedged snugly where the lower canyon narrows, about ½ mile above the Millard Canyon picnic area. The short canyon-bottom walk is shaded most of the way by huge canyon oaks and a handful of tall alders and willows. Only a short distance from Altadena, this makes an ideal Sunday-afternoon saunter.

Description

Drive up Chaney Trail Drive in Altadena. Continue over the ridge and down to the parking area at the bottom of Millard Canyon.

Pass a locked gate and proceed a hundred yards up the fire road to Millard Canyon Public Campground. At the upper end of the campground, a wooden sign points right (east) to Millard Canyon Falls. Follow the shady canyon trail ½ mile to the foot of the falls. Don't try to climb over the falls; people have been injured attempting this dangerous feat. Return the way you came. ▲

21 Brown Mountain Loop—Millard Canyon to Tom Sloan Saddle, Brown Mountain, Brown Mountain Fire Road, back to Millard Canyon

HIKE LENGTH:	12 miles round trip; 2500' elevation gain
CLASSIFICATION:	Strenuous
SEASON:	November-May
TOPO MAP:	Pasadena

Features

The "Brown Boys"—Owen and Jason—were familiar figures in and around the foothills of the front range back in the 1880s. These long-bearded sons of fiery pre-Civil War abolitionist John Brown lived in a small log cabin near the head of El Prieto Canyon, a beautiful wooded glen between the Arroyo Seco and Millard Canyon. Great lovers of nature, the "boys" (both were well past middle age) spent much time exploring the neighboring mountains. As a monument to their famous father, they sought out a mountain peak to name in his honor. After an abortive attempt to place his name on what later became known as Mount Lowe, they settled on the long, rounded mountain rising high between Millard Canyon and Bear Creek. Today it is still known as Brown Mountain.

This lengthy loop trip climbs up Millard Canyon to Tom Sloan Saddle (named for a former district ranger), traverses the 4485' hog-back of Brown Mountain, and descends from the west ridge around the south slope back to the starting point. You should be in good physical condition for this one, and since part of the loop is trailless, wear lug-soled boots.

Description

From Loma Alta Drive in Altadena, turn north on Chaney Trail Drive and follow it to the junction atop Sunset Ridge; turn right and park outside the locked gate blocking the Sunset Ridge fire road. Hike up the Sunset Ridge fire road about 400 yards to a distinct but unmarked trail leading left, around the ridge into Millard Canyon above the falls (see Trip 19). Follow the streamside trail, hopping boulders where the footpath has been washed out, to the Dawn Mine. Continue up canyon another ½ mile, then follow the recently reworked trail (courtesy of the JPL Hiking Club) as it crosses to the left side of the creek and climbs out of the canyon. (Millard Canyon curves east beyond here; if you miss the turnoff and start walking east, backtrack 200 yards.) Follow the brush-cleared trail as it zigzags north up to Tom Sloan Saddle, 3½ miles from the start. Here you stand on the divide between Millard Canyon and Bear Creek, a three-way trail junction (see Trip 33). From the saddle, leave the trail and scramble left (west) up the firebreak and a faint hikers' footpath, climbing over or around three false summits, to the true hogback summit of Brown Mountain, slightly more than a mile.

Standing on the bare summit, you are rewarded with a superb panorama of the front range. To the west, across the yawning chasm of the Arroyo Seco, is Mt. Lukens. Northward, beyond Bear Creek and the upper Arroyo Seco, are the impressive humps of Josephine and Strawberry Peaks. Eastward are the triumvirate of San Gabriel Peak, Mt. Markham, and Mt. Lowe. And to the south, past Millard Canyon, sprawls the megalopolis, usually half hidden in brown murkiness.

When you're through looking, continue west along the fire break, dropping 1600' in 2 miles to the upper end of the Brown Mountain Fire Road (closed to public vehicles). Proceed down the fire road as it curves southeastward around the lower slopes of Brown Mountain. Go left (east) at all road junctions. After 6 miles, the fire road reaches the Millard Canyon Public Campground. Since your car is up on Sunset Ridge (unless you arranged a car shuttle), you'll have to climb 400' up the other side of the canyon. At the lower end of the campground, take the unmarked trail that leads left from the fire road and climbs to the ridgetop just above the parking area. ▲

22 Sunset Ridge via old railway bed to Mount Lowe Campground

HIKE LENGTH: 11 miles round trip; 2400' elevation gain
CLASSIFICATION: strenuous (1 day); moderate (2 days)
SEASON: November-May
TOPO MAPS: Pasadena, Mt. Wilson

Features

The Mount Lowe Scenic Railway was one of the 19th century's engineering marvels, visited by tens of thousands during its 43 years of operation (1893-1936). This trip climbs the Sunset Ridge Trail, above Millard Canyon, to the old railway bed near what was once called the

Cape of Good Hope. It then follows the railway bed, now the Sunset Ridge-Mount Lowe fire road, to the Mount Lowe Tavern site, presently Mount Lowe Trail Camp. The old railway bed is gently graded and offers a splendid panorama over mountain, canyon and lowland—particularly on a clear winter or spring day when air pollution does not muddy the sky. You will pass some of the "stations" denoting historic sites on the old railroad, erected by the Forest Service in 1977 but unmaintained in recent years.

You can make this a strenuous one-day trip or stay overnight at Mount Lowe Campground, making it a very pleasant two-day outing. Note: The water at Mount Lowe Trail Camp is at this writing unsafe for drinking without treatment. Check with the Forest Service for latest water condition.

Description

From Loma Alta Drive in Altadena, turn north on Chaney Trail Drive and follow it to the ridgetop junction; turn right and park outside the locked gate blocking the Sunset Ridge fire road. Do not block the road.

Walk past the locked gate and up the fire road about 400 yards to a junction on your left. Take the trail, which contours around the ridge above Millard Canyon. Just before you reach the canyon bottom is a trail junction. Go right (the left branch goes up Millard Canyon) and follow the trail all the way up to the top of Sunset Ridge, 2½ miles, where you rejoin the fire road. As you proceed up the fire road, Echo Mountain and its historic ruins come into view down to your right. In

Sunset on Mt. Lowe

½ mile you meet the old railway bed coming up from Echo Mountain. Just beyond you pass a metal post (the first of the "stations") on your left, indicating that you have reached Cape of Good Hope, where the mountain railroad rounded a point above Millard Canyon.

Over the next mile you pass the Dawn Mine Trail, leading left down into Millard Canyon (recently restored and an option on your return trip), and the landmarks of Dawn Mine Station, Grand Circular Bridge and Horseshoe Curve as the route climbs high along the east wall of Millard Canyon. Finally the old roadbed turns east, passes through Granite Gate, ascends to near the head of Grand Canyon and reaches Mount Lowe Trail Camp, on your left, 5½ miles from the start. The shady trail camp—on the site of old Mount Lowe Tavern—is equipped with tables, stoves and restrooms, but no good water unless it is treated. You may wish to continue up the roadway, then right at a junction, out to Inspiration Point, ½ mile from the campground. Here, on clear days, you are rewarded with a grand view down Castle Canyon to Echo Mountain and beyond over the lowlands to the distant sea.

Return the same way, or descend via Castle Canyon or the Upper Sam Merrill Trail to Echo Mountain (described in Trip 23), then go up the lower part of the railway bed to Sunset Ridge and return the way you came. Another option is to return the way you came, down the old roadbed, until you turn down the Dawn Mine Trail to Dawn Mine in Millard Canyon (see Trip 19). Any of these alternatives adds about 2 miles to the round trip. ▲

23 Mount Lowe Railway Loop Tour— Altadena to Echo Mountain, old railway bed, Mt. Lowe Trail Camp, Inspiration Point, Castle Canyon, back to Echo Mountain and Altadena

HIKE LENGTH: 12 miles round trip; 2800′ elevation gain

CLASSIFICATION: Moderate

SEASON: November-May

TOPO MAPS: Pasadena, Mt. Wilson

Features

The old Mount Lowe Railway is long gone, remembered only by those who traveled in these mountains during the early decades of the century. Yet once it attracted tourists by the thousands. No visit to Southern California was complete without taking in the thrilling ride up the cable incline to Echo Mountain, then the twisting trolley trip to rustic Ye Alpine Tavern, nestled deep in a forest cove on the slopes of Mt. Lowe. When the mountain railway was built, it was considered one of the engineering wonders of the world.

The Mt. Lowe Railway and resort complex was the idea of two visionary Pasadenans—Civil War balloonist and inventor Thaddeus S. C. Lowe, and engineer David J. Macpherson. With Lowe supplying the capital and Macpherson directing operations, the railway was hacked out of the mountainside in three stages during 1892 to 1895. First was a trolley line from Altadena into Rubio Canyon, where the first of Lowe's popular edifices—Rubio Pavilion—was located (see Trip 25). Then an incline railway climbed 1300' to Echo Mountain, where two hostelries—The Chalet and Echo Mountain House—were perched (see Trip 24). Finally, a 4-mile winding trolley ride, past airy viewpoints such as Horseshoe Curve, Cape of Good Hope, Grand Circular Bridge and Granite Gate, carried awestruck visitors to Ye Alpine Tavern (later called Mt. Lowe Tavern). Lowe was bankrupted by the venture, and for most of the 43 years of its operation, the Pacific Electric Railway Company ran the complex. From its opening in 1893 until the burning of Mt. Lowe Tavern in 1936, an estimated 3,100,000 persons visited the renowned mountain railway and resort complex.

Above Echo Mountain, the scars of the winding railway are clearly visible today, and it is possible to hike to the tavern site along its broken bed, the upper section of which is now part of the Sunset Ridge-Mt. Lowe fire road (see Trip 22). At the old tavern site, under spreading oaks and spruces, the Forest Service has constructed the Mt. Lowe Trail Camp, with tables, stoves, rest rooms and a spring-fed drinking fountain.

A half mile out from the trail camp, overlooking the San Gabriel Valley, is the Ramada at Inspiration Point, where tourists took in the view that was described in Mt. Lowe Railway days as "breathtaking, beautiful, inspiring."

In the last several years, much restoration work has been accomplished by weekend volunteers of the Scenic Mt. Lowe Historical Committee. Old trails have been cleared, artifacts have been uncovered and placed on display at Echo Mountain, and—their crowning achievement—the ramada at Inspiration Point was rebuilt and dedicated on November 16, 1996.

For those with vivid imaginations, it is possible to stand among the foundations of the mountain railway and picture oneself a part of Professor Lowe's dream-come-true. This loop trip is for those with such imaginations.

Description

Drive to the north end of Lake Avenue in Altadena and park along-side the road. To your right (east), marked by a sign painted on a stone pillar, is the beginning of the Sam Merrill Trail to Echo Mountain.

Follow the trail east, down across Las Flores Canyon, and up the slopes to Echo Mountain (see Trip 24). From Echo Mountain, turn north and follow the broad, graded railway bed around the head of Las Flores Canyon to Sunset Ridge, where you pick up the Sunset Ridge-Mt. Lowe fire road. Turn right (north) and proceed up the recently improved fire road. Within the next mile, you pass such viewpoints of yesteryear as Cape of Good Hope, Horseshoe Curve, and most famous of all, Grand Circular Bridge. There is no bridge here now, just a sharp hairpin turn of the road. After following the slope above Millard Canyon for a mile, you round the mountain and turn east high above Grand Canyon, passing through the remains of the rock outcropping once known as Granite Gate. Four miles from Echo Mountain, you finally reach Mt. Lowe Trail Camp, nestled in a grove of oak and spruce. The stone wall foundation just east of camp is all that remains of old Mt. Lowe Tavern.

From the trail camp, continue up the fire road, going right (south-east) at a road junction, ½ mile to the ramada at Inspiration Point. Immediately east of the point is an unmarked trail dropping into Castle Canyon. Follow this narrow trail as it zigzags steeply down through spruce- and oak-shaded Castle Canyon, around the head of Rubio Canyon, where you cross a small creek (usually water), and over to Echo Mountain again, 2 miles. Then descend the Sam Merrill Trail to Altadena.

An alternate route between Echo Mountain and Mt. Lowe Trail Camp is the old Sunset Trail (shown on the topo map as a continuation of the Sam Merrill Trail). Both ends are unmarked, but not difficult to find. From Echo Mountain, it starts up the crest of the ridge directly to the north, zigzags up and around what was known in Mt. Lowe Railway days as Sunset Point, turns east, paralleling the old railway bed about 200' above it, and intersects the Mt. Lowe fire road about 300 yards south of the trail camp. To locate the trail from above, follow the fire road 300 yards south from Mt. Lowe Trail Camp to a road junction; the trail goes right (west) just south of the junction. This Sunset (or Upper Sam Merrill) Trail is regularly maintained by volunteers from Altadena and other nearby communities. ▲

24 Sam Merrill Trail— Altadena to Echo Mountain

HIKE LENGTH:	5 miles round trip; 1400' elevation gain
CLASSIFICATION:	Moderate
SEASON:	November-May
TOPO MAPS:	Pasadena, Mt. Wilson

Features

If it were not for the efforts of a handful of public-spirited and sentimental Pasadena and Altadena citizens, the Mount Lowe Railway would be all but forgotten today. These people have given freely of their time and effort in restorative projects, enabling today's visitor to relive some of this bygone era when cable cars and trolleys climbed high on the mountain.

One of these volunteer efforts was the construction and maintenance of the Sam Merrill Trail from Altadena to Echo Mountain. The trail was built during the '30s by Charles Warner and the Forest Conservation Club of Pasadena to replace the original, overgrown footpath. During the '40s it was maintained and improved by Samuel Merrill of Altadena, retired clerk of the Superior Court of Los Angeles. After Merrill's death in 1948, the pathway was named in his honor. Today it is kept in good condition by the Altadena Trail Blazers, a group of high school and college students who care about their local mountains.

Back in the early years of the Mount Lowe Railway, Echo Mountain was known as "The White City." Perched on top were two hotels— Echo Mountain House and The Chalet—a powerhouse, a machine shop, a dormitory, a reservoir, a small zoo, the Mt. Lowe Observatory and, so it would not be forgotten after dark, the world's most powerful searchlight. All but the searchlight were painted white, clearly visible from the valley below. To reach the White City, tourists were hoisted up the cable incline in "White Chariots."

Through a series of fires and windstorms, the White City was destroyed—Echo Mountain House first (1900), then all but the observatory (1905), and finally the observatory itself (1928). The incline was abandoned in 1938.

Nothing but ruins remain today. To commemorate what once was here, a bronze plaque is embedded in cement next to the old incline bullwheel. Among the foundations, young Coulter pines and incense cedars, planted by conservation groups in 1941 and 1948, are growing tall.

This trip takes you up the Sam Merrill Trail to Echo Mountain, gives you a guided tour of where once stood the White City, and returns you the same way.

Description

Drive to the north end of Lake Avenue in Altadena and park alongside the road. To your right (east), marked by a sign painted on a stone pillar, is the beginning of the Sam Merrill Trail to Echo Mountain.

Follow the trail east alongside a fence, then down across Las Flores Canyon, and up the east slope of the canyon. After three zigzagging miles, you reach the ridge behind (north of) Echo Mountain. Here you intersect the old railway bed (see Trip 23). Turn right (south) and follow the railway bed about 100 yards to the Echo Mountain ruins. You come first to the commemorative plaque and the old incline bullwheel, embedded in cement. Just beyond, the wall on your left is the foundation of Echo Mountain House, and the pile of concrete rubble ahead is what remains of the incline depot and powerhouse, dynamited by the Forest Service in 1959. From the steps of Echo Mountain House, you can look directly down the incline bed, descending 1300' into Rubio Canyon. (Do not descend the incline; footing is loose and it is dangerous.) East of the Echo Mountain House site, 100' down the ridge, is the site of the Chalet. Nothing remains of this first hotel. The Mt. Lowe Observatory, housing a 13-inch telescope, was located behind Echo Mountain, ¼ mile up the ridge. Directly below the observatory was the reservoir. (Several sections of the trail were washed out following the Pinecrest fire in 1979 and heavy rain in February 1980. Volunteer work has now made the trail passable, but proceed with care. In the event new washouts occur on the precipitous middle section, proceed directly up the ridge from the powerline crossing, halfway up, to Echo Mountain, steep but not difficult.) ▲

25 Altadena to Rubio Canyon

HIKE LENGTH: 1½ miles round trip; 200' elevation gain
CLASSIFICATION: Easy
SEASON: November-May
TOPO MAP: Mt. Wilson

Features

Rubio Canyon was once one of the premier scenic attractions of the San Gabriel Mountains, visited by thousands of tourists.

For 43 years, from 1893 to 1936, Rubio Canyon was an important way-station on the Mt. Lowe Railway. Tourists rode the winding electric trolley into the canyon, then climbed aboard the "White Chariots" for the thrilling ride up the cable incline to Echo Mountain. During the initial 16 of those years, Professor Lowe's elegant Rubio Pavilion stood at the foot of the incline. Set amid a forest garden of sycamores, live oaks, ferns, and wildflowers, the pavilion was a beauty to behold. Radiating up and down canyon from the edifice were more than a mile of planked walks and rustic stairways, leading through a picturesque setting of ferns, mossy nooks, and miniature waterfalls. All this came to an end in 1909, when a severe thunderstorm sent huge boulders crashing down upon the pavilion, demolishing the double-decked structure and causing the only death in all the years of the Mt. Lowe operation. From then until the railway's end, Rubio Canyon was nothing but a transfer point for passengers bound for Mt. Lowe Tavern.

Today, this scene is difficult to visualize. Absolutely nothing remains of the magnificent pavilion that once spanned the canyon. The lower end of the incline has been completely eroded, and all the rails have been removed.

Sadly, man's recent folly has almost totally destroyed the quiet charm of Rubio Canyon. In 1998, workers hired by the Rubio Canyon Land and Water Association tried to reroute a water pipe damaged in the 1994 Northridge earthquake. The pipe supplied water to about 200 homes below the canyon. While carving a notch in the steep canyonside, the workers accidentally triggered an avalanche that buried the little waterfalls and cascades under thousands of tons of boulders and debris.

The accident embarrassed the Forest Service and outraged environmentalists, who are demanding that the 100-foot-deep pile of rocks be removed. But federal officials say the cleanup is not their responsibility and the tiny water company that owns the pipeline says it doesn't have the funds to pay for it. As a result, the landslide has triggered a number of lawsuits and legal claims.

Ordinarily, we would remove this trip in view of the vast destruction in the canyon. As of this writing (November 1999), no efforts have been made to remove the mass of boulders and restore Rubio Canyon's beauty. Hopefully, restoration work will begin sometime in the near future. With this in mind, we are continuing to list this once pleasant walk.

Description

Drive up Rubio Canyon Road in Altadena. Turn left (west) on Rubio Crest, then right (north) on Rubio Vista and follow the latter one block to its junction with Pleasant Ridge Drive. Notice a narrow dirt path between the two houses on the corner, leading north into Rubio

Canyon. Just beyond the houses lies the old railway bed that once took passengers to Rubio Pavilion.

Proceed along this eroded bed, mostly easy going but difficult in two spots where the trestle is gone and you must cross small gullies. In ½ mile you round a bend and run out of roadway; just beyond is the site of Rubio Pavilion and the foot of the cable incline. Just ahead lies the monstrous pile of boulders and debris, completely covering most of the miniature waterfalls of Mt. Lowe Railway days. The huge mass is unstable so do not attempt to climb over it.

After your sad rendezvous with history, return the same way. ▲

26   Altadena to Henninger Flats

HIKE LENGTH: 5 miles round trip; 1400' elevation gain
CLASSIFICATION: Moderate
SEASON: November-June
TOPO MAP: Mt. Wilson

Features

Above Altadena, the scars of the old Mt. Wilson Toll Road are clearly visible, zigzagging sharply up the chaparral-covered mountainside from the mouth of Eaten Canyon. About a third of the way up can be observed a rather conspicuous forested bench. This is Henninger Flats (sometimes incorrectly spelled "Henniger Flats"), home of the Los Angeles County Experimental Forestry Nursery.

The flats have a rich history. They were originally homesteaded by "Captain" William K. Henninger, who grew hay, corn, vegetables, fruit and melons on his "farm in the clouds." In the early 1900s the flats were leased to the Forest Service and, under the guidance of Theodore P. Lukens, the first scientific reforestation experiments in California were conducted. Thousands of seedlings from the nursery here were transplanted to fire-blackened slopes all over Southern California.

Since 1928 Henninger Flats and the surrounding slopes have been under the administration of Los Angeles County foresters. Until the devastating fire of 1993, the flats produced almost 120,000 new tree seedlings each year knobcone pine, Coulter pine, Canary Island pine, Monterey pine, Aleppo pine, and varieties of cypress, cedar, and sequoia. The nursery is making a comeback, but it will be some time before the fire-charred slopes are again verdant. Fortunately, most of the nursery buildings escaped destruction. A new administration building with a museum on the ground floor, open to the public on weekends, displays reforestation and historical exhibits. A picnic area and public campground, set amid trees that were not burned, are maintained by the county.

Description

Drive to the beginning of the old Mt. Wilson Toll Road at the east loop of Pinecrest Drive in Altadena.

Walk past the locked gate, down across Eaten Canyon, and up the cypress-rimmed old road, zigzagging up steep chaparral-covered slopes 2½ miles to Henninger Flats. Just inside the shady flats, on both sides of the road, are the picnic and campground. Straight ahead is the new administration building and museum. Behind the museum and to the right are the structures of the county reforestation nursery. A fire lookout tower, formerly atop Castro Peak in the Santa Monicas, stands as a historical exhibit to your left.

Return the same way you came. Do not try shortcuts down the chaparral-blanketed slopes.

Other options are to continue up the toll road to Mt. Wilson (see Trip 27), or follow the Idlehour Trail into upper Eaten Canyon (see Trip 28). ▲

Mt. Wilson Toll House and Road (1914)   Pasadena Historical Society

27 Mt. Wilson Toll Road— Altadena to Mt. Wilson or Mt. Wilson to Altadena

HIKE LENGTH:	9 miles each way; 4500' elevation gain or loss
CLASSIFICATION:	Strenuous (uphill), Moderate (downhill)
SEASON:	November-June
TOPO MAP:	Mt. Wilson

Features

Back in the 1920s, when the age of the automobile arrived in Southern California, the Mt. Wilson Toll Road was a favorite of strong-nerved drivers. Narrow, zigzagging, cliff-hanging much of the way, without side rails, this auto route from Altadena to the summit of Mt. Wilson often saw heavy holiday traffic. For those who preferred not to drive themselves, there was the popular Mt. Wilson Stage, making the upward grind twice a day—more often when the traffic demanded. Surprisingly, there were few accidents. Evidently the obvious dangers served as a cautioning influence. The most amazing episode in the road's long history was the Altadena-Mt. Wilson automobile race, held several times during the '20s, a contest that makes the more famous Pikes Peak road race pale by comparison. The record for the 9-mile, 4500', 44-hairpin-turn event was 22 minutes flat, set by Pasadenan Frank Benedict in 1922, driving a Paige 6-66.

It was the Pasadena and Mt. Wilson Toll Road Company, incorporated 1889, that first envisioned a road to the mountaintop. Two years later the company completed a four-foot-wide toll trail to the summit—50¢ per rider, 25¢ per hiker. Not until 1907 was the trail widened to a 10-foot roadway, this to transport the 60-inch telescope to its mountaintop home. In 1912 the toll road was widened to 12' to accommodate the 100-inch telescope and was opened to the public, and for the next 24 years it was a popular Sunday drive except among the faint-of-heart. The end for this historic old route came in 1936. Superseded by the new Angeles Crest Highway, it was closed to the public and turned over to the Forest Service for use as a fire road. So it remains today.

Mt. Wilson, home of one of the world's great observatories, is probably the best-known mountain in Southern California. It was named for Benjamin Wilson, who built the first modern trail to its summit in 1864 (see Trip 39). The first telescope on the peak was the 13-inch refractor of the short-lived Harvard Observatory, 1889-1890. Since 1904, the famed Carnegie Observatory has been here, thanks to the enthusiasm and efforts of two far-seeing men—astronomer George Ellery Hale and businessman-turned-philanthropist Andrew Carnegie. From its installation in 1917 until surpassed by the 200-incher on Mt. Palomar in 1946, the 100-inch Hooker reflector on Mt. Wilson was the world's largest. Today the Mt. Wilson and Mt. Palomar observatories-recently renamed the Hale Observatories—are operated jointly by the Carnegie Institution and Cal Tech.

In 1948 television came to Mt. Wilson in the form of transmitting stations for all seven Los Angeles channels. Mt. Wilson's natural flora was supplemented by a manmade forest of antennas, towers and domes, most of them visible from the valley below. Television not only came, it conquered. In 1964 Metromedia Inc., operators of Station KTTV, purchased the entire mountaintop from the old Mt. Wilson Hotel Company. The rambling old hotel, a fixture on the mountain since 1915 (a previous hotel was built in 1905, and burned in 1913), was torn down and in its place arose Skyline Park, complete with a pavilion, a children's zoo, and neat picnic areas. Metromedia deeded the mountaintop to the Forest Service in 1976. Old-timers would hardly recognize the mountaintop today.

You can do the old toll road in two ways. The easier is to have someone drive you to Mt. Wilson (19 miles from La Canada), then hike down. Much more strenuous is to hike up the road from Altadena. Either way, you are rewarded with a close-at-hand view of the abrupt, chaparral-coated south slope of the front range, and you will marvel at the fortitude and backbone of those who once drove this tortuous roadway to the sky.

Prof. Lowe (center) and party on Mt. Lowe (1892)

Description

To walk up the old toll road, drive to the lower entrance, guarded by a locked gate, at the east loop of Pinecrest Drive in Altadena.

Proceed along the dirt roadway down across the mouth of Eaten Canyon and 2½ miles up to Henninger Flats (see Trip 26). The only water enroute is here at these lushly forested flats, so fill up. Continue on the road through the flats and up around a ridge. In another mile you pass the junction of the Idlehour Trail (see Trip 28), and just beyond, the site of George Schneider's old Halfway House, where perspiring travelers once enjoyed shade and refreshment. The toll road then zigzags up the ridge, rounds the south and east slopes of Mt. Harvard, and reaches the Harvard-Wilson Saddle, site of old Martin's Camp (see Trip 34), 8 miles from Altadena. One more uphill mile and you gain the Mt. Wilson Road just west of the entrance to Skyline Park.

If you prefer to hike down the toll road, drive up the Angeles Crest Highway to Red Box, 14 miles from La Canada, then go right on the Mt. Wilson Road to the parking area just outside the entrance to Skyline Park, 5 more miles. Immediately south of the parking area is the upper end of the old toll road, marked by a wooden sign. ▲

28 Altadena to Henninger Flats, Idlehour Trail to Eaton Canyon, Idlehour Trail Camp, Inspiration Point, Castle Canyon, Echo Mountain, back to Altadena

HIKE LENGTH:	13 miles round trip; 4100' elevation gain
CLASSIFICATION:	Strenuous
SEASON:	November-May
TOPO MAPS:	Mt. Wilson, Pasadena

Features

Few San Gabriel canyons compare with Eaton in ruggedness and inaccessibility. Precipitous sidewalls plunge down from lofty ridges to make this V-shaped gorge in the heart of the front range. A tumbling stream hurries down the length of the chasm, finally to plunge over idyllic Eaton Falls just above the canyon's mouth. The upper end of the canyon widens into a broad basin under the towering white faces of Mt. Markham and San Gabriel Peak.

Trails into Eaton Canyon have always been difficult to build and maintain, because of the rugged terrain. In decades past, you could hike directly up the canyon on a narrow footpath that clung to the side of the gorge above the stream, but the Pasadena Water Department fence has closed this approach. Today you avoid the difficult lower gorge by utilizing the Mt. Wilson Toll Road to climb above the canyon, then drop into its more gentle upper reaches via the Idlehour Trail.

You reach the canyon bottom at Idlehour Trail Camp, a secluded spot of unusual natural charm. Here the creek experiences one of its few serene moods, and a fine forest of oak, bay and big-cone spruce provides cover. In this woodsy haunt once stood Camp Idle Hour, a small trail resort of the Great Hiking Era. The name signified the quiet, restful mood of the place, and throughout its existence (1915-1929) the camp was a favorite of lovers of sylvan seclusion.

The trip is a rather long one, involving much up and down, as all visits into upper Eaton Canyon must. But it samples some of the most scenic country in the front range. With a 2-mile car shuttle, your itinerary follows a great loop, dropping into Eaton Canyon from the east and climbing out via the west slope. If a car shuttle is not available, you can retrace your steps, covering just half of the loop. In any event, be in top shape; it's an all-day hike for most people.

Description

Leave one car at the Sam Merrill Trail entrance, at the head of Lake Avenue in Altadena. Drive the other to the beginning of the Mt. Wilson Toll Road, where Pinecrest Drive makes its east-end loop.

Walk up the old toll road, passing Henninger Flats. One mile beyond the Flats, look for the Idlehour Trail leading left, marked by a small wooden sign. Follow the trail over a slight rise and steeply down to Idlehour Trail Camp in Eaton Canyon. The camp, on a bench just east of the stream, is a good picnic or overnight spot, equipped with tables and stoves.

From Idlehour Trail Camp the trail goes upstream, passing the foundations of several old cabins. Much of the path here is washed out and you must boulder-hop. In ½ mile from the trail camp, look for the trail leaving the left side of the creek bed—it's easy to miss. The pathway turns sharply left (west), zigzags steeply up and around a ridge, contours into a side canyon (usually a small trickle of water), and continues up to meet a spur of the Mt. Lowe fire road, 3 miles. Turn left (southeast) on the spur road to the cement foundation of old Inspiration Point, about 200 yards. Just east of the point is an unmarked trail dropping down Castle Canyon (see Trip 23). Follow this trail down to Echo Mountain, then the Sam Merrill Trail (see Trip 24) to Lake Avenue in Altadena, 5 miles downhill all the way.

The Pinecrest fire of September 1979 burned much of Eaton Canyon, but the chaparral has rapidly grown back. ▲

29 Red Box to San Gabriel Peak, Mt. Disappointment

HIKE LENGTH:	7 miles round trip; 1400' elevation gain
CLASSIFICATION:	Moderate
SEASON:	All year
TOPO MAPS:	Chilao Flat, Mt. Wilson

Features

Mt. Disappointment (5994') stands high on the crest of the front range, but not quite as high as its next-door summit, San Gabriel Peak. Hence the "disappointment" when some government surveyors lugged their equipment to the top in 1875, then had to continue to the higher summit to do their surveying.

This trip follows the new San Gabriel Peak Trail, built by the JPL Hiking Club in 1988, then the upper end of the Mt. Disappointment fire road to gain the San Gabriel Peak-Mt. Disappointment saddle, and then climbs both peaks. The views from both summits are panoramic.

Description

Drive up the Angeles Crest Highway from La Canada to Red Box, 14 miles, then turn right onto the Mt. Wilson Road. Follow the latter about one-third mile to the beginning of the Mt. Disappointment fire road on your right. Park here, but don't block the roadway.

Take the new San Gabriel Peak Trail, which begins about 50 feet to the left (east) of the fire-road gate. The trail switchbacks up, under a canopy of big-cone spruce and live oak, to a junction with the upper section of the Mt. Disappointment fire road, 1 mile. Proceed up the fire road to the ridgetop, 200 yards. Take the trail left, which drops 50 feet to the San Gabriel Peak-Mt. Disappointment saddle, then climbs the west ridge of San Gabriel Peak to the summit, ½ mile.

On your return, follow the fire road to the summit of Mt. Disappointment, ¼ mile. The top is cluttered with electronic installations and empty buildings dating from the 1950s, when an Army Nike missile station was located here.

Descend the way you came up. An option, adding a mile to the trip, is to follow the fire road down. Or, if you can arrange a 8-mile car shuttle, descend the trail from the San Gabriel Peak-Mt. Disappointment saddle to Markham Saddle and on to the Mt. Wilson Road at Eaton Saddle (see Trip 32). ▲

30 Eaton Saddle to Markham Saddle, Mt. Lowe

HIKE LENGTH: 3 miles round trip; 500' elevation gain
CLASSIFICATION: Easy
SEASON: November-June
TOPO MAP: Mt. Wilson

Features

This is the easy way to do historic Mt. Lowe. You start from the backside—the Mt. Wilson Road—and contour across the white diorite cliffs of San Gabriel Peak to Markham Saddle, then climb the gentle north slope of the mountain through fire-thinned chaparral and clusters of small oak trees to the bare summit.

In the early days it was called Oak Mountain, for the groves of splendid live oak on its upper slopes. By this name it was known when Professor Thaddeus Sobieski Coulincourt Lowe and a party of leading Pasadena citizens ascended it on horseback in 1892. Lowe was showing his friends his proposed mountain railway, then just beginning construction. One of the party proposed the name "Mount Lowe" in honor of the man in their midst. The motion was carried by a chorus of ayes, and in the words of publicist and writer G. Wharton James, "There, above the clouds it was named and will continue to be named when every one of the party present at the christening shall have been laid away in mother earth, and generations yet unborn will trace its rugged outlines on their physical geographies and call it Mt. Lowe."

Lowe planned to continue his mountain railway to the top and construct there a summit hotel, but he ran out of funds after reaching the site of Ye Alpine Tavern 1000' below. During the years of the Mt. Lowe Railway, untold thousands climbed to the top via two well-graded trails from the tavern. On the summit was a small, open observation pavilion and a series of view tubes pointed at various attractions below.

With the burning of Mt. Lowe Tavern in 1936 and the abandoning of the mountain railway, visits to Mt. Lowe almost ceased, and the trails and summit paraphernalia fell into decay. In recent years, a party of Sierra Club volunteers has restored one of the trails, polished and relettered the old view tubes, and left a new register book with pictures of the Mt. Lowe of old. Old Mt. Lowe is again worth visiting.

Description

Drive up the Angeles Crest Highway 14 miles from La Canada to Red Box. Turn right on the Mt. Wilson Road 2½ miles to Eaton Saddle. The saddle is unnamed on maps but easy to locate; it is the first spot past Red Box where the highway touches the top of the ridge and you can look south.

Walk past the locked gate onto the Mt. Lowe fire road, overlooking the yawning chasm of upper Eaton Canyon. Follow the road as it turns west and contours around the precipitous south face of San Gabriel Peak. Near midpoint, the road tunnels through a nearly vertical cliff. Notice the old guard rails outside the wall, remnants of the airy old Cliff Trail that once joined Mt. Lowe Tavern with Mt. Wilson. After a short mile you reach Markham Saddle, a V-shaped cleft between San Gabriel Peak and Mt. Markham. Here you leave the road and take an unmarked footpath to the left that leads southwest around the slopes of Mt. Markham. You cross an area of sparse growth, where fire a few years ago took its toll, to the saddle between Mt. Markham and Mt. Lowe, then enter a forest of small oaks as the trail rounds the east slope of Mt. Lowe. About 300 yards beyond this last saddle, look for an unmarked side trail branching back to your right (west). Leave the main trail (which continues down to Mt. Lowe Trail Camp (see Trip 31 and walk up the side footpath about ¼ mile to the bare summit of Mt. Lowe.

After enjoying the fine vista over the front-range country and pondering the history of this place, return the way you came. ▲

31   Eaton Saddle to Mt. Lowe Trail Camp, Mt. Lowe Fire Road back to Eaton Saddle

HIKE LENGTH: 6 miles round trip; 700′ elevation loss and gain
CLASSIFICATION: Moderate
SEASON: November-June
TOPO MAP: Mt. Wilson

Features

This loop trip takes you completely around Mt. Lowe and visits secluded Mt. Lowe Trail Camp, once the location of famed Mt. Lowe Tavern (see Trip 23). Most of the hike is via easy-graded fire road but about two miles are on the historic, oak-shaded Mt. Lowe "East" Trail, recently reworked into good condition. You are rewarded enroute with superb vistas down into Eaton, Bear, and Grand canyons and, if the atmosphere is clear, down the south slope of the front range to the sprawling San Gabriel Valley.

Description

Drive up the Angeles Crest Highway 14 miles from La Canada to Red Box. Turn right on the Mt. Wilson Road 2½ miles to Eaton Saddle.

Walk past the locked gate and follow the Mt. Lowe fire road to Markham Saddle, then turn left on the Mt. Lowe East Trail to the saddle between Mts. Markham and Lowe (see Trip 30 for details). Continue on the trail through a shady oak forest around the east shoulder of Mt. Lowe, then down around the south slope via switchbacks to a badly eroded fire break. The trail crosses the fire break and continues zigzagging down to the Mt. Lowe fire road. Follow it south 100 yards to a junction with the Inspiration Point spur road, then right about 300 yards to Mt. Lowe Trail Camp. Here, under oak and spruce, there are tables, stoves, rest rooms, and a spring-fed drinking fountain. The stone foundation adjacent to the camp is all that remains of old Mt. Lowe Tavern, once the scene of much merrymaking.

To return, retrace your steps up the fire road to the Inspiration Point junction. Go left and follow the road northwest around Mt. Lowe's long west ridge, then east back across Markham Saddle and San Gabriel Peak's white cliffs to Eaton Saddle.

An option is to return via the Old Mount Lowe "West" Trail, recently reworked and put into fine condition by the JPL Hiking Club. You will be delighted to come across several of the old view tubes—iron pipes aimed at landmarks below—placed along the trail some sixty years ago. About 300 yards up the Mt. Lowe fire road from the Inspiration Point spur road—almost directly north of and above Mt. Lowe Trail Camp—the trail zigzags up the west slope of a ravine, then contours around the hillside to your left, paralleling the fire road about 200 feet above it. (The trail you see climbing to the right, also reworked by the JPL Hiking Club, connects with the Mount Lowe "East" Trail.) You contour and climb westward ½ mile, passing several of the old view tubes, then round the ridge and ascend steadily east, with two switchbacks near the top, to Mt. Lowe's bare summit. From the summit, descend the beaten path back to the Mount Lowe "East" Trail (see Trip 30),then walk left to Markham Saddle and via the fire road back to Eaton Saddle. ▲

32 Eaton Saddle to Markham Saddle, San Gabriel Peak

HIKE LENGTH: 3½ miles round trip; 1000' elevation gain
CLASSIFICATION: Moderate
SEASON: November-June
TOPO MAP: Mt. Wilson

Features

Pyramidal San Gabriel Peak towers high on the crest of the front range. From its 6161' summit, you get an unmatched 360-degree panorama over the wrinkled San Gabriel Mountains, with the front range in the foreground, laced as it is with paved highways, fire roads, trails, fire breaks, and assorted paraphernalia of mankind. Your vista is good because the top is tall, small and apical. As on nearby Strawberry Peak (Trip 36), you get that airy, top-of-the-world feeling.

There are days—increasing in number—when you look down upon canyon-ascending arms of smog, rising from the vast megalopolis dimly visible to the south. There are other days when billowing clouds swirl around you, playing hide-and-seek with nearby peaks. And there are those rare winter and spring days when the sky has been washed

Switzer Camp north of falls

David Allen James

clean by storm, and you can see half of Southern California spread out in stark beauty. These are the days to climb San Gabriel Peak.

This climb is short in distance, but the trail is steep and narrow in spots, so wear lug-soled boots.

Description

Drive up the Angeles Crest Highway 14 miles from La Canada to Red Box. Turn right up the Mt. Wilson Road to Eaton Saddle, 2½ miles. The saddle is unmarked on maps but easy to locate: it is the first spot after Red Box where the highway touches a gap in the ridge and you can look south.

Walk past the locked gate and across the rugged south face of San Gabriel Peak via the Mt. Lowe fire road ½ mile to Markham Saddle. At the saddle, just beyond the water tank, turn sharp right (north) and pick up a brushy, unmarked trail leading up the mountainside. Follow the trail up one switchback, then across the west slope of San Gabriel Peak to the high saddle between Mt. Disappointment and San Gabriel Peak, about ¾ mile. Part of this pathway is eroded where it crosses the steep slope, so watch your step. At the saddle, turn right (east) and follow a steep climbers' trail up the ridge to the top.

After enjoying your eagle's-view, return the way you came. Do not try to descend directly down the ridge (southeast) to Eaton Saddle—the footing is unstable and the chaparral is thick and thorny. ▲

33 Eaton Saddle to Markham Saddle, Tom Sloan Saddle, Bear Canyon, Arroyo Seco, Switzer Campground

HIKE LENGTH: 10 miles round trip; 2500' elevation loss, 700' gain

CLASSIFICATION: Moderate

SEASON: November-June

TOPO MAPS: Mt. Wilson, Pasadena, Condor Peak

Features

This trip is a long walk through some of the most scenic parts of the front-range country. The first 8 miles are all downhill, the last 2 uphill. One may especially enjoy the descent of Bear Canyon to the middle gorge of the Arroyo Seco via the remnant of the old Tom Sloan Trail, an historic footpath that once joined two of the most popular resorts in the mountains—Mt. Lowe Tavern and Switzer's. With the demise of the Tavern in 1936, the trail fell into disuse and now much of it is overgrown, but the stretch through Bear Canyon remains passable, although partly washed out. A car shuttle between Eaton Saddle and Switzer Picnic Area, 6 miles apart on the Angeles Crest Highway, is required.

Description

Drive up the Angeles Crest Highway 10½ miles from La Canada, to the side road down to Switzer Picnic Area, ½ mile past the junction of the Angeles Crest and Angeles Forest highways. Turn right and descend ¼ mile to the parking area outside the Picnic Area. Leave one car here. Drive the other 4 miles up the Angeles Crest to Red Box, then go right 2½ miles on the Mt. Wilson Road to Eaton Saddle.

Walk past the locked gate, following the Mt. Lowe fire road across the face of San Gabriel Peak to Markham Saddle, then on down the road until it reaches the top of Mt. Lowe's long west ridge, 1¾ miles from the start. Here the road switches back eastward. Leave the road here and proceed down the obvious but unmarked trail on the right (north) side of the ridge to Tom Sloan Saddle, ¾ mile. From the saddle, follow the old Tom Sloan Trail as it drops northwest down into Bear Canyon. You reach the canyon floor in ½ mile, a beautiful spot shaded by big-cone spruce.

The foundations you see are all that remain of several old cabins, abandoned after a fire many years ago. Continue down Bear Canyon, following the streamside trail, or boulder-hopping where the trail has been washed out, to Bear Canyon Trail Camp, located on a spruce-shaded bench on the south side of the creek, about two miles from Tom Sloan Saddle. Here is a perfect lunch stop, as it lies about halfway on your trip.

After lunch, continue down-canyon, partly on trail, partly boulder-hopping, to the junction with the Arroyo Seco, 2 more miles. Turn right (north) up the Arroyo Seco and follow the trail past the delightful pools and cascades of the middle gorge to a difficult-to-spot junction where the trail climb s out of the canyon to the main Arroyo Seco Trail above Switzer Falls (see Trip 17 for description of this part). If you reach the foot of Switzer Falls, you've gone ¼ mile too far up the canyon. (Under no circumstances should you try to climb over the falls.) When you reach the main Arroyo Seco Trail high on the ridge, turn right (north) and follow the well-beaten footpath through Commodore Switzer Trail Camp and on to Switzer Picnic Area (see Trip 17). ▲

34 Mt. Wilson to Harvard-Wilson Saddle, Mt. Harvard

HIKE LENGTH:	2½ miles round trip; 800′ elevation gain
CLASSIFICATION:	Easy
SEASON:	November-June
TOPO MAP:	Mt. Wilson

Features

This short trip samples the upper reaches of the old Mt. Wilson Toll Road, visits the site of once-famous Martin's Camp on the Harvard-Wilson Saddle, and climbs to the easy summit of Mt. Harvard. It is a pleasant Sunday afternoon stroll, and rewards you with superb vistas of the rugged canyon-and-spur country of the San Gabriels' abrupt south slope.

Few who stride across the Harvard-Wilson Saddle enroute to "bag" Mt. Harvard are aware that they are treading over the site of old Martin's Camp, once a popular mountain resort—before the Mt. Wilson Hotel made obsolete all adjacent hostelries of a more primitive nature. The tent camp was founded by Pasadena restaurateur Peter Steil in 1889 to take advantage of the publicity over the installation of the Harvard telescope on Mt. Wilson. Two years later Steil sold out to Clarence Martin. Under Martin the pine-shaded resort reached its zenith of popularity, and until well into this century, seldom was the camp not filled on summer weekends. Today nothing remains but the low stone retaining walls, built by Martin in 1892, and four full-grown Monterey pines planted as seedlings about 1894.

In 1892 President Charles W. Eliot of Harvard University, during a visit to Mt. Wilson, was escorted to the top of a promontory just south of camp. As a tribute to Dr. Eliot, the peak was christened "Mt. Harvard" by the escorting party of distinguished Pasadena citizens.

Description

Drive to the parking area just outside the entrance to Mt. Wilson's Skyline Park, 18 miles from La Canada. Immediately south of the parking area is the upper entrance to the old toll road, marked by a wooden sign. Proceed down the road ¾ mile to Harvard-Wilson Saddle, where you will want to pause to search out the signs of old Martin's Camp—retaining walls, little flat benches, Monterey pines.

There are two ways to climb Mt. Harvard, both easy. You can follow the Harvard spur road up from the saddle to a point just beyond (south of) the peak, then north 100 feet to the cleared summit. Or you can take Martin's old trail up, partly overgrown but still passable after a half century of disuse. To locate this historic pathway, proceed up the Harvard spur road about 200' on your right a black arrow on a rock points out the beginning of the trail. 100' up the trail is a small flat with three power poles where the footpath appears to terminate; scramble up to your left about 30' to regain the trail and follow it through pines and occasional brush to the summit.

Return to Mt. Wilson the same way. ▲

35 Josephine Fire Road to Josephine Peak

HIKE LENGTH:	6 miles round trip; 1900' elevation gain
CLASSIFICATION:	Moderate
SEASON:	All year
TOPO MAP:	Condor Peak

Features

5558' Josephine Peak, the high point of the prominent spur extending two miles west from Strawberry Peak, offers superb views of the Big Tujunga watershed. A well-graded fire road climbs 3 miles from the Angeles Forest Highway to the fire lookout on the summit. This makes for a pleasant stroll when the weather is mild. Don't try it on a hot day: except for a few forested spots near the top, the route is devoid of shade. An option, if you are in top physical condition, is to climb both Josephine and Strawberry peaks by this approach, descending either the same way or via Colby Canyon (see Trip 36).

The origin of the name "Josephine" is obscure. As early as 1889 there was a Josephine Gold Mine in the upper Big Tujunga. Several authorities believe the peak was named for the wife of J. B. Lippencott, USGS surveyor who used the summit as a triangulation point while mapping the mountains in 1894. Another source claims it was named for the daughter of Phil Begue, one of the early forest rangers in the range. The fire lookout, erected in 1937, burned down in the 1976 Big Tujunga fire. It will not be replaced.

Description

From La Canada, drive up the Angeles Crest Highway 10 miles to the junction with the Angeles Forest Highway, opposite the Clear Creek Ranger Station. Park off the highway alongside the ranger station.

The Josephine fire road begins on the east side of the Angeles Forest Highway about 50 yards north of the junction. Walk past the locked gate up the road. The route climbs the ridge dividing Colby Canyon from Clear Creek and zigzags to the crest of Josephine's east ridge, 2 miles. Here is a junction right (east) to Josephine Saddle and Strawberry Peak (see Trip 36) and left (west) to Josephine Peak. Go left, following the road through oaks and spruces on the north side of the ridge, to the concrete foundation of the summit lookout.

Return by the same route or, if you can arrange a 1-mile car shuttle, descend to Josephine Saddle and down the old Colby Canyon Trail to the Angeles Crest Highway (see Trip 36). Don't take trailless shortcuts that may look tempting; the chaparral is thick and thorny. ▲

36 Colby Canyon to Strawberry Peak

HIKE LENGTH: 6 miles round trip; 2600' elevation gain

CLASSIFICATION: Moderate

SEASON: All year

TOPO MAPS: Condor Peak, Chilao Flat

Features

Highest of all summits of the front range of the San Gabriels is Strawberry Peak, a lump-shaped mass of granite boulders rising 6164' above sea level. Looming far above the Angeles Crest Highway between the Arroyo Seco and Big Tujunga watersheds, its airy crown commands a sweeping vista over mountain and lowland.

Strawberry is the only peak in the front range whose ascent involves more than a plodding walk-up. Its nearly vertical upper ramparts give you a taste of the alpinist's exhilaration, and once on top you'll really know that you've climbed a mountain. There, with slopes tapering precipitously on all sides, you get that top-of-the-world feeling. Many hikers consider it the "fun peak" of the San Gabriels.

The peak was labeled by wags at Switzer's Camp back in the 1880s, who fancied a resemblance to a strawberry standing on its stem. It has been a popular climb as long as modern man has trod the San Gabriels. During the Great Hiking Era (1895-1938), knapsackers chugging over the well-beaten trail between Switzer's and Colby's often made the airy side-trip to take in the rewarding summit panorama. It is just as frequented today. Every fair-weather weekend finds climbers by the score testing their stamina and skill on its steep granite spine.

The climb is not particularly difficult for those in good physical condition who have had some experience on class 3 rock. Using proper caution—testing hand and foot holds and moving slowly—you should have little trouble if you follow the route indicated by green arrows painted at intervals on boulders. Lug-soled boots are strongly recommended. Extra care should be taken on the descent, for that is when most accidents occur.

Description

Drive up the Angeles Crest Highway to the Colby Canyon parking area, 11 miles from La Canada and 1 mile beyond the Angeles Crest-Angeles Forest Highway Junction.

Proceed up the Colby Canyon trail, which starts on the left (west) side of the creek. This trail is one of the historic pathways of the range. It is passable, although eroded in some spots and brushy in others. The trail follows the creek for ¼ mile, then climbs steeply up the right side to bypass several small waterfalls where the canyon narrows. You then drop back into the shady, alder-filled upper canyon before switchbacking up through thorny chaparral to Josephine Saddle, 2 miles from the highway. Here you meet the Strawberry Spur of the Josephine fire road. An alternate way to reach this saddle—½ mile longer but easier going—is to follow the fire road from Clear Creek Ranger Station (see Trip 35).

From Josephine Saddle, the old Colby Trail winds eastward, around the north flank of Strawberry Peak and down to Strawberry Meadow (see Trip 38). Do not take this trail; instead climb eastward up a steep climbers' path that ascends the crest of the ridge. About ¼ mile above Josephine Saddle you must negotiate a rocky section of about 75 vertical feet, before continuing along the ridgecrest ¾ mile to the base of Strawberry Peak's imposing granite summit block. Here the faint-of-heart will turn back; the route looks more difficult than it actually is and has some exposure. Follow the faded green arrows painted at intervals on the rock face, gripping firmly and testing hand and foot holds, to the final summit ridge, then scramble a hundred feet to the top. ▲

37 Red Box to Strawberry Peak, Josephine Saddle, Colby Canyon

HIKE LENGTH: 7 miles round trip; 1500′ elevation gain
CLASSIFICATION: Moderate
SEASON: All year
TOPO MAPS: Chilao Flat, Condor Peak

Features

This trip climbs Strawberry Peak by the east slope—the easy way—then continues down the precipitous west face to Josephine Saddle and Colby Canyon via the standard route (see Trip 36). If you are unfamiliar with third-class rock scrambling, don't do the whole traverse—return from the peak to Red Box, the same way you came. For the entire traverse here described, a car shuttle between Red Box and Colby Canyon-4 miles apart on the Angeles Crest Highway—is required. The hike and the peak scramble, staying high on the ridge most of the way, offer panoramic vistas over the front range and the Upper Big Tujunga-Alder Creek backcountry. Wear lug-soled boots; much of the peak climb and descent is an off-trail scramble over granite boulders.

Strawberry Peak from back side

Description

Drive up the Angeles Crest Highway to Colby Canyon, 11 miles from La Canada and 1 mile beyond the Clear Creek junction. Leave one car here and drive the other vehicle to Red Box Ranger Station, 4 miles farther up the highway.

Cross the Angeles Crest Highway and follow it northeast about 50 yards to the beginning of the Barley Flats fire road. Turn left (north) and proceed up the fire road. In ½ mile you will come to a trail leading up to the left. Follow this path up to the ridge just south of Mt. Lawlor, then pick up an obvious but unmarked trail that contours around the mountain, high above the Angeles Crest Highway, to the saddle between Lawlor and Strawberry Peak—2 miles from the start. From the saddle, turn left (northwest) and follow a faint climbers' pathway up the ridge, through chaparral and over boulders, to the summit—800' gain in ¾ mile.

Descend the abrupt west face, following the green arrows painted on the rocks, then continue down the ridge to Josephine Saddle and descend Colby Canyon to the Angeles Crest Highway (see Trip 36 for route description). If you don't like the west face's steep rock descent, return to Red Box the way you came. ▲

38 Red Box to Strawberry Spring, Strawberry Meadow

HIKE LENGTH:	8 miles round trip; 1400' elevation gain
CLASSIFICATION:	Moderate
SEASON:	All year
TOPO MAP:	Chilao Flat

Features

The backside of Strawberry Peak holds pleasant surprises. Close under granite cliffs and boulder-stacked ridges, springs seep cold water and little meadows sprout tall grasses. In the protective shade of the great mountain, forest and chaparral intermingle and grow lush and green. Here, just across the ridge from the busy Angeles Crest Highway, away from ranger stations and public campgrounds and the assorted miscellany that accompanies civilization, you savor a small touch of wilderness.

This delightful trail trip takes you over the mountain from Red Box to Strawberry Meadow—three small meadows close below the great north cliff of Strawberry Peak. You pass alternately through clusters of dense chaparral—scrub oak, manzanita, snow brush, mountain mahogany—and a varied forest of live oak, big-cone spruce and Jeffrey and Coulter pine. The footpath that winds through this wilderness garden is old and little-traveled, making it all the more appealing. Bring lunch and a good book—you'll want to stay awhile. Unfortunately the area was burned in the 1979 Mill Creek fire, but Strawberry Meadow is gradually regaining its old charm.

Description

Drive up the Angeles Crest Highway to Red Box Ranger Station, 15 miles above La Canada. Cross the Angeles Crest Highway and follow it northeast about 50 yards to the beginning of the Barley Flats fire road. Follow the road ½ mile, then turn left and follow the trail up to the ridge and around the mountain to the saddle between Mt. Lawlor and Strawberry Peak (see Trip 37).

From the saddle, continue on the trail as it gently descends around the east and northeast slopes of Strawberry Peak. The first ¼ mile is in fine shape; beyond, the path is narrow and eroded in spots but not difficult to follow. You pass through alternate stretches of chaparral on sun-exposed slopes and forest on shady north faces. About a mile from the saddle you enter a woodsy recess and reach Strawberry Spring— flowing icy cold in spring and early summer. Then you cross a ridge and get your first glimpse of the lower meadow of Strawberry Meadow, with the great north cliff as an imposing backdrop. The trail drops steeply into a forested gully below the meadow and continues over another low ridge and down to Colby Ranch, a retreat for young Methodists. You don't go that far.

Just beyond the low point where the trail crosses the forested gully, look for a side trail marked with red-paint arrows on rocks leading back to the left (southwest). Turn sharp left and follow this footpath to the lower meadow of Strawberry Meadow, about ¼ mile. You can stop here and enjoy the grassy clearing surrounded by oak and spruce and boulder ridges, or you can continue up the red-marked trail another ½ mile, past a second small meadow, to the westernmost and largest clearing, right beneath the towering granite cliffs. Here, under magnificent Coulter pines, are two picnic tables placed by young Methodists from Colby Ranch.

After you've fully savored this delightful sanctuary, you have three options. The easiest is to return to Red Box the way you came. Or you can continue on down to Colby Ranch, if you have arranged a car shuttle and have permission of the operators of this private retreat. Or—if you can arrange a car shuttle—you can take the recently rebuilt Colby Trail, which leaves Strawberry Meadow near its upper (southwest) edge and climbs westward, then contours the north slope around to Josephine Saddle, 2 miles. From here you can descend the Colby Canyon Trail to the Angeles Crest Highway (see Trip 36). ▲

39 Sierra Madre to Orchard Camp

HIKE LENGTH:	9 miles round trip; 2000' elevation gain
CLASSIFICATION:	Moderate
SEASON:	November-May
TOPO MAP:	Mt. Wilson

Features

Beautiful Little Santa Anita Canyon is steeped in history. Ages before the arrival of the white man, Gabrielino Indians forged a rough footpath up the canyon and on to Mt. Wilson. Benjamin Wilson, proprietor of the Lake Vineyard Rancho in what is now San Marine and a prominent Southern California citizen, built the first modern trail into the San Gabriels up this canyon in 1864 to obtain timber from the mountaintop that was subsequently named in his honor. In 1889 the Harvard University telescope was toted up this trail piece by piece, to occupy the first observatory on Mt. Wilson.

In a secluded glen, shaded by giant canyon oaks and big-cone spruce, near the head of the main canyon, "Don Benito"—as Wilson was known to his many California friends—built his "Halfway House" in 1864. This original Halfway House, so named because it was midway between Sierra Madre and Mt. Wilson, was a construction camp for the original Mt. Wilson Trail. Later it was homesteaded by two colorful mountaineers, George Aiken and George Islip, who planted a small grove of apple, cherry, plum and chestnut trees. With the maturing of these trees, the place became known as Orchard Camp. Around 1890 James McNally made Orchard Camp into a trail resort, and for fifty years this sylvan hostelry, under a succession of owners, was one of the most popular in the range. Its peak year was 1911, when over 40,000 persons signed the camp register. Orchard Camp was abandoned in 1940. Today the buildings and tents are gone. But the enchanting streamside spot still holds appeal for lovers of sylvan seclusion.

Today, most of Little Santa Anita Canyon lies within the Sierra Madre Historical Wilderness Area, owned by the city of Sierra Madre. For years, Ambrose Zaro, "the grand old man" of the trail, has almost single-handedly maintained it. His death in March 1990 was mourned by all Mount Wilson 'Frail hikers.

Our very pleasant trail trip follows this historic footpath from Sierra Madre to old Orchard Camp and back. Take along a picnic lunch and a camera; you'll be so delighted by the woodsy charm of Orchard Camp you'll want to stay awhile.

Description

Drive to the junction of Mira Monte Avenue and Mt. Wilson Trail Drive in Sierra Madre. Do not leave your car above the immediate area of the junction; Mt. Wilson Trail Drive is a private road.

Proceed about 150 yards up Mt. Wilson Trail Drive to the new beginning of the Mt. Wilson Trail, marked by a large wooden sign on the left. Follow the trail alongside some private homes up to the ridgetop road, where the main footpath begins. Pass the locked gate and continue up the trail as it climbs steadily along the west slope of the canyon, far above the stream. In 1½ miles you reach a junction. The main trail goes straight ahead, staying high above the stream, climbing steadily. The trail branching right drops to the creek (the site of old Quarterway House), then follows the stream up-canyon, fording the creek twice before climbing to rejoin the main trail in 1 mile. Go either way.

A short distance beyond where the trails rejoin, you round a ridge and enter the welcome shade of a live-oak forest. The trail climbs steadily for another mile, then drops to the small creek trickling down from Decker Spring. Beyond, you climb steeply, then contour ½ mile through cool forest to Orchard Camp, located on an oak- and spruce-shaded bench just above the sparkling creek. The huge canyon-oak tree here is one of the oldest and largest oaks in the range. (A core test places its age at 1,500 years.)

Return the way you came. ▲

40   Old Mt. Wilson Trail— Sierra Madre to Mt. Wilson

HIKE LENGTH:	7½ miles one way; 4500' elevation gain
CLASSIFICATION:	Strenuous (uphill), Moderate (downhill)
SEASON:	November-May
TOPO MAP:	Mt. Wilson

Features

This original trail up Mt. Wilson—forged by Benjamin Wilson in 1864—has, over the years, been one of the premier attractions in the range. No trail in the range has a richer heritage. (Its early history, an integral part of the Little Santa Anita Canyon story, is told in Trip 39.) During the Great Hiking Era (1895-1938), the dusty pathway vibrated under the tramp of boots and the pounding of hooves every fair-weather weekend. Every Saturday morning, hundreds would disembark from the red Pacific Electric trolley cars in Sierra Madre, knapsack slung o'er shoulder, and ramble up the crowded footpath to the mountaintop resorts. Sunday afternoon, often weary and foot-sore, the hikers would emerge from the mountains to find the big red cars waiting, ready for the homeward journey.

With the end of the hiking era and the distraction of World War II, the old Mt. Wilson Trail fell into years of disuse. Gradually it became overgrown and badly eroded in spots. In 1953 UNSAFE TO TRAVEL signs were posted at both ends of the historic pathway. Fortunately, a group of Sierra Madre volunteers, led by Bill Wark, spent many weekends restoring the trail, and it was reopened in 1960. The late Ambrose Zaro maintained the trail for 30 years before his death in 1990.

Description

Drive to the junction of Mira Monte Avenue and Mt. Wilson Trail Drive in Sierra Madre. Leave your car in the immediate area of the junction, not up on Mt. Wilson Trail Drive.

Walk about 150 yards up Mt. Wilson Trail Drive to the new beginning of the trail, marked by a large wooden sign. Then follow the trail to Orchard Camp, 4½ miles (see Trip 39). Be sure to fill your canteen at Orchard Camp; this is the last dependable water. Follow the trail as it climbs steeply through chaparral, oak and spruce up the west slope of Little Santa Anita Canyon, crosses the canyon near its head, and switches back eastward to the firebreak atop the ridge separating Little Santa Anita from Winter Creek. Here you intersect the Winter Creek Trail (see Trip 44). Turn left (west) and continue up the trail as it zigzags steeply up to the Mt. Wilson Toll Road, 2 miles from Orchard Camp. Turn right and follow the old toll road through an open forest of bigcone spruce to its junction with the Mt. Wilson Road just outside the entrance to Skyline Park, 1 mile. ▲

41 Chantry Flat to Sturtevant Falls

HIKE LENGTH: 3 miles round trip; 500′ elevation gain
CLASSIFICATION: Easy
SEASON: November-June
TOPO MAP: Mt. Wilson

Features

Although there are many cascades and small water drops in Big Santa Anita, Sturtevant Falls is the only real waterfall in the canyon. Its silver spray plunges fifty feet into a shallow, rock-ribbed pool, shaded by alders and oaks. Enroute you pass through a beautiful grove of oaks and ferns at the site of old Fern Lodge. In spring, there are fine displays of wildflowers, particularly prickly phlox and sticky monkey flower.

This is a short, leisurely stroll from Chantry Flat, a good beginner's hike. You can combine the trip with a picnic under the oaks at Chantry Flat, where there are stoves, tables and water.

Description

From the Foothill Freeway in Arcadia, take the Santa Anita Avenue off-ramp and drive north to Chantry Flats, 6 miles.

Take the Gabrielino Trail, which descends from the entrance to Chantry Flats into Big Santa Anita Canyon. Cross the Winter Creek Bridge and walk up the broad canyon trail, passing numerous private cabins, to a three-way trail junction. Continue straight ahead. You ford Big Santa Anita Creek in 200 yards, then reford where the canyon makes a sharp bend leftward. Scramble over boulders the last 100 yards to the large pool at the foot of the falls.

Please do not attempt to climb the falls; people have been injured trying to do so.

Return the way you came. ▲

42 Chantry Flat to Spruce Grove Trail Camp

HIKE LENGTH:	8 miles round trip; 1400' elevation gain
CLASSIFICATION:	Moderate
SEASON:	November-June
TOPO MAP:	Mt. Wilson

Features

Big Santa Anita Canyon is one of the most beautiful wooded glens in the San Gabriels, a favorite sylvan retreat for nature-lovers, hikers and campers. Under its spreading evergreens, the musical waters of Big Santa Anita Creek reveal a delightful diversity of moods—now dancing merrily over pebble-strewn floor, then pausing in limpid pool, only to plunge headlong over waterfall and cascade to begin a new cycle. Along the banks sprout regal woodwardia, dotted here and there in springtime with clusters of lupine, larkspur and other flowering herbs, all contributing to nature's soft picture of elegance.

Detracting somewhat from the primeval scene are the dozens of check dams, built of precast concrete and interlocked like giant Lincoln logs, which have converted the once-rustic canyon bottom into a progression of artificial stair-steps, with glassy sheets of water pouring over ten- to twenty-foot drops. These check dams were constructed by the Los Angeles County Flood Control District and the Forest Service in the early 1960's as safeguards against erosion, much to the disgust of conservationists. Fortunately, twenty years of nature's regrowth have softened the appearance of artificiality, and the canyon has regained much of its former beauty.

Big Santa Anita has a rich history. In the 1850s there was a gold strike in the lower canyon, just about where Santa Anita Dam and Reservoir are now. The excitement lasted a few years, then the miners drifted away. In 1886-87 the Burlingame brothers constructed a rough road along the west slopes of the canyon to Winter Creek, intent upon hauling out timber to fire their charcoal kilns. But the San Gabriels were declared a timber reserve before the brothers could cut any trees. In the 1890s Wilbur M. Sturtevant, one of the real pioneers in the range, hewed out his famous trail to the head of the canyon, where he set up Sturtevant's Camp, long one of the most popular trail resorts in the mountains. Others followed "Sturde." To cater to the swarms of hikers who visited the canyon every weekend, a host of trail hostelries were

Sturtevant's Camp—early days   Huntington Library

established—Joe Clark's Halfway House; First Water Camp, where the trail over the ridge from Sierra Madre first touched the stream; Roberts' Camp, at the junction of Big Santa Anita and Winter Creek; Fern Lodge and the Sierra Club's Muir Lodge below Sturtevant Falls; and Hoegee's Camp halfway up Winter Creek. All these old camps except Sturtevant's, which is now a church retreat, are gone today.

This very pleasant trip takes you through the lushly forested heart of Big Santa Anita, passing the sites of many of the historic hostelries, to Spruce Grove Trail Camp in the upper canyon.

Description

From the Foothill Freeway in Arcadia, take the Santa Anita Avenue off-ramp and drive north to Chantry Flat, 6 miles.

To the right of the road as you enter Chantry Flat you will notice a locked gate and a paved fire road descending into the canyon. A large sign proclaims this road THE GABRIELINO RECREATION TRAIL (see Trip 47) and gives trail mileages. Follow this fire road to the canyon bottom, ½ mile, cross the Winter Creek bridge, and walk up Big Santa Anita Canyon on the broad trail, passing numerous check dams and private cabins. About ½ mile farther you enter a shady recess and pass a cluster of cabins, once the site of Fern Lodge. Just beyond, the trail forks three ways: straight ahead to Sturtevant Falls (Trip 41), left and then sharp right up the slope to climb above the falls into the middle canyon, and sharp left up the hillside to the upper canyon. Either of the latter two trails may be taken; they rejoin in a mile. The leftmost one is easier walking, while the middle path directly above the falls and through the scenic middle section of the canyon is more beautiful. In 1½ miles you drop back beside the alder- and spruce-shaded stream and reach Cascade Picnic Area, on a forested bench to the right of the creek. Continue up the trail as it climbs the east slope, then drops to ford the creek and ascends to Spruce Grove Trail Camp, ¾ mile farther. There are stoves and tables here, the only place in the canyon where you can legally camp. (If possible, do this trip on a weekday; weekends usually find Spruce Grove crowded with Boy Scout campers.)

Return the way you came. ▲

43 Chantry Flat via Sturtevant Trail to Hoegee Trail Camp, Mt. Zion, Big Santa Anita Canyon

HIKE LENGTH:	10 miles round trip; 1800' elevation gain
CLASSIFICATION:	Moderate
SEASON:	November-June
TOPO MAP:	Mt. Wilson

Features

This very attractive circle hike follows the old Sturtevant Trail, known today as the Upper Winter Creek Trail, from Chantry Flat to Hoegee Trail Camp, then climbs over Mt. Zion Saddle and drops into upper Big Santa Anita Canyon. You then follow the canyon trail down past Sturtevant Camp, Spruce Grove Trail Camp, and Cascade Picnic Area to lower Winter Creek, then climb back up to Chantry Flat. This is a delightful circle trip—one of the best in the San Gabriels—passing across chaparral-coated slopes with expansive canyon views, through lush conifer forest and streamside woodland, alongside bubbling creeks, fully sampling the grandeur of the Big Santa Anita watershed.

Wilbur Sturtevant, known as "Sturdy" to his friends, built his trail from Sierra Madre over the ridge into Big Santa Anita Canyon, then along the west slope to his resort camp in 1896. For decades, the famous Sturtevant Trail felt the trod of many boots and the joyous voices of legions of hikers bound for the delights of Big Santa Anita and its many hostelries of the "Great Hiking Era." One who hiked the Sturtevant Trail and fell in love with spruce-and-fern-lined Winter Creek was Arie Hoegee, who built his resort camp there in 1908. For three decades it was a favorite destination for hikers. The rustic buildings are long gone, but the Forest Service has made the little streamside glen into Hoegee Trail Camp, with stoves and tables. Hoegee's Camp has an unusual distinction: in the 24-hour period January 22-23, 1942, a total of 26.12 inches of rain fell here, establishing a Southern California record that still stands.

Description

From Foothill Freeway in Arcadia, take the Santa Anita Avenue off-ramp and drive north to Chantry Flat, 6 miles.

From the upper parking area at Chantry Flat, take the fire road that begins to the left (south) of the ranger station, adjacent to the sloping picnic area. After ¼ mile, at the road's second switchback, turn right onto the Upper Winter Creek Trail, indicated by a wooden sign. Follow the trail as it climbs, contours, and then drops along the west wall of Big Santa Anita Canyon, mostly through chaparral, passing a Mt. Wilson trail junction, to Winter Creek, in 2 miles. Your trail fords Winter Creek, briefly climbs and then drops to another trail junction. For Hoegee Trail Camp, go right; the trail refords Winter Creek and reaches the spruce-shaded camp after a few minutes' walk. (An option that cuts your hiking distance in half is to descend the Winter Creek Trail to the Big Santa Anita Canyon Trail, then turn right and climb back up to Chantry Flat.)

To continue on the full circle trip, retrace your steps from Hoegee Trail Camp back up to the Mt. Zion Trail junction, marked by a small sign. Go right and follow the newly restored Mt. Zion Trail (which is really the upper section of the old Sturtevant Trail) as it climbs, first through forest and then chaparral, to Zion Saddle, 1¼ miles. A side trail right leads ¼ mile to Mt. Zion's summit and spectacular views over the Big Santa Anita watershed. Your main trail then gently descends through lush forest, mostly big-cone spruce, to a junction with the Big Santa Anita Canyon Trail, ¾ mile. Turn right and descend the canyon trail, fording the creek twice, to Spruce Grove Trail Camp, ½ mile. Your trail descends to Cascade Picnic Area, contours the mountainside, drops to Winter Creek, and climbs back up to Chantry Flat (see Trip 42 for a full description).

Note: This circle trip was made possible by the restoration of the Mt. Zion section of the Sturtevant Trail by Howard Casey, Chris Kasten and Bohdan Porendowski of Camp Sturtevant in 1976-79, and "The Big Santa Anita Gang" and Sierra Club volunteers in 1984-85. ▲

44 Chantry Flat to Mt. Wilson via Winter Creek

HIKE LENGTH: 6 miles one way; 3600' elevation gain

CLASSIFICATION: Strenuous

SEASON: November-June

TOPO MAP: Mt. Wilson

Features

Mt. Wilson can be climbed by trail from more directions than any other peak in Southern California. The mountain is laced with foot-paths.

This trail goes from Chantry Flat over the old Sturtevant Trail to Winter Creek, then climbs steeply up through a dense forest of big-cone spruce and oak to the Winter Creek-Little Santa Anita divide, where it joins the Old Mt. Wilson Trail and continues on to the toll road and the summit. A number of interesting variations can be planned— see below. Be in top physical shape; the trip is steeply uphill most of the way.

Description

From the Foothill Freeway in Arcadia take the Santa Anita Avenue off-ramp and drive north to Chantry Flat, 6 miles.

Walk from the parking area up to the Chantry Flat Ranger Station and start up the fire road that begins 50 feet left (south) of it, adjacent to the sloping picnic area. After a short ¼ mile, at the road's second switchback, turn right (northwest) onto the Sturtevant Trail (marked UPPER WINTER CREEK TRAIL on the topo map) and follow it around the ridges 1½ miles to a trail junction where a sign indicates Mt. Wilson. If you reach Winter Creek above Hoegee Trail Camp, you've gone 100 yards too far. Turn left (northwest) at the junction and follow the trail as it climbs steeply for 2 miles through spruce and oak to the ridgetop and a second trail junction. Here you intersect the Old Mt. Wilson Trail coming up from Little Santa Anita Canyon (see Trip 40). Continue up the ridgetop trail as it zigzags steeply up, back and forth across the fire break, to the Mt. Wilson Toll Road, ½ mile farther. Turn right and follow the old toll road 1 mile through open stands of spruce to its junction with the Mt. Wilson Road just outside the entrance to Skyline Park.

You have several options on this trip. You can descend the way you came up. You can have someone awaiting you at the road loop outside Mt. Wilson Skyline Park to drive you down. You can descend the old toll road to Altadena (see Trip 27) or the Old Mt. Wilson Trail via Little Santa Anita Canyon to Sierra Madre (see Trip 40)—both of these options require a car shuttle. Or you can enter Skyline Park (refreshments available), walk past the observatory grounds to the east end of the mountain and descend via the Sturtevant Trail (see Trip 45). ▲

45   Chantry Flat to Sturtevant Camp and Mt. Wilson

HIKE LENGTH:	8 miles one way; 3900′ elevation gain
CLASSIFICATION:	Strenuous
SEASON:	November-June
TOPO MAP:	Mt. Wilson

Features

The canyon of Big Santa Anita cuts a deep semicircular groove into the south flank of the front range, its head lying close under the precipitous east slope of Mt. Wilson. An old trail travels most of the length of the canyon, then switchbacks steeply up forest and chaparral slopes to the mountaintop. For many years the pathway was overgrown and eroded, but recently it has been reworked and put in good condition—steep, but easily passable.

This trip follows this old route, traveling up-canyon from Chantry Flat to Sturtevant Camp, then climbing right up the mountainside to Echo Rock and the observatory grounds. It is long and it is tiring; be in top shape. For the descent, you have a number of options—see below.

Clouds over southeast ridge of Mt. Wilson   Huntington Library

Description

From the Foothill Freeway in Arcadia take the Santa Anita Avenue off-ramp and drive north to Chantry Flat, 6 miles.

Take the fire road that descends from near the entrance of Chantry Flat into Big Santa Anita, then follow the canyon trail to Spruce Grove Trail Camp, 4 miles (see Trip 42). Your trail climbs above the camp, fords the stream, and reaches a trail junction, the right fork going up to Newcomb Pass and on into the West Fork country (see Trip 46). Go left above the creek, and almost immediately you reach the woodsy haunt of Sturtevant Camp, operated as a Methodist Church retreat. Just before entering the camp, your trail turns sharply left and crosses the creek just above a debris barrier. You now leave the canyon and switchback steeply up through dense forest cover, which thins as you get higher, to Echo Rock at the east end of the Mt. Wilson summit plateau, 8 miles from Chantry Flat. Walk through the observatory grounds to Skyline Park.

From the summit you have several options. You can descend the way you came. You can cross the Mt. Wilson Observatory grounds and Skyline Park to the one-way, out-only gate at Skyline Park entrance and have someone waiting for you at the road loop. You can descend the old toll road to Altadena (see Trip 27) or the Old Mt. Wilson Trail via Little Santa Anita Canyon to Sierra Madre (see Trip 40)—both of these options require a car shuttle. Or you can descend the Winter Creek Trail back to Chantry Flat (see Trip 44). This last alternative is suggested; it makes an interesting and strenuous circle trip with no car shuttle. ▲

46 Chantry Flat to Newcomb Pass, West Fork of the San Gabriel River, Devore Trail Camp, West Fork Campground

HIKE LENGTH: 9 miles one way; 2300′ elevation gain

CLASSIFICATION: Strenuous

SEASON: November-June

TOPO MAP: Mt. Wilson

Features

Big Santa Anita was once *the* gateway into the San Gabriel backcountry, before the Angeles Crest Highway tamed the range and forever changed it. Anglers, hunters and adventurers by the score tramped up the Sturtevant Trail, over the divide at Newcomb Pass, and into the wild interior of the range.

In 1896 Wilbur Sturtevant completed his trail into his resort camp near the head of the canyon. Louie Newcomb, another mountain pioneer who had settled in Chilao around 1888, decided "Sturde's" footpath would make an excellent first leg for trips into his beloved backcountry So with the help of 10 laborers, Louie thrashed out a rough pathway over the divide that now bears his name—Newcomb Pass—and down into the West Fork, then up Shortcut Canyon and on to his Chilao country. While Louie was working on his path, Sturtevant and several others incorporated the "Sierra Madre and Antelope Valley Toll Trail" and charged 25¢ per person to hike across the range to the desert, with the first fares going to Newcomb for his part in building the trail. However, Louie, who had to do the collecting himself, complained that no system of collecting would work without a man on the trail at all times, and "that don't pay wages, so I had to quit it." So passed a brief and colorful episode in the story of San Gabriel trails. Although the toll was abandoned, the trail remained, and for three decades—until the completion of the Angeles Crest in the mid-'30s—it was a major thoroughfare for backcountry ramblers.

Today, a network of paved highways and unpaved byways provides easy access to the mountain regions behind Mt. Wilson. The once-vital trail over Newcomb Pass is virtually unused. But this pathway hewed by Louie Newcomb three quarters of a century ago remains; in fact it has recently been worked and is in good condition.

This trip leads to no wild mountain recesses as it once did, but it traverses some scenic chaparral and pine country in its long course from Chantry Flat over the historic divide and down to old West Fork Campground. From there, you have a number of interesting options—described below.

Description

From the Foothill Freeway in Arcadia, take the Santa Anita Avenue off-ramp and drive north to Chantry Flat, 6 miles.

Take the fire road that descends from near the entrance of Chantry Flat into Big Santa Anita, then follow the canyon trail to Spruce Grove Campground, 4 miles. Less than ½ mile beyond the campground, just before you reach Sturtevant Camp, is a trail junction. Go right (northeast) up the slope and around the chaparral-rich ridges to Newcomb Pass, a long 2 miles (a sign at the pass says 3). Here you meet a fire road coming in from the east; do not take it. Continue north on the trail, switchbacking down through a forest of spruce and oak and crossing the Rincon-Red Box fire road after a short ¼ mile, for 2 miles to Devore Trail Camp on the West Fork. From here it's a shady mile upstream to the West Fork Campground and the dirt road coming down from Red Box.

You now have a number of options. You can return the way you came. You can walk a mile up the road toward Red Box, then take the Rattlesnake Trail up Mt. Wilson (see Trip 50) and descend back to Chantry Flat via either the trail down the head of Big Santa Anita (see Trip 45) or the toll road-Winter Creek Trail (see Trip 44). Or, you can continue on the route of Louie Newcomb and the back-country pioneers, taking the trail up Shortcut Canyon to the Angeles Crest (see Trip 52), then down into the upper Big Tujunga, up to Charlton Flat and on to Chilao. This totals 18 miles, suggesting an overnight stay at either Devore or West Fork Campground. ▲

47 Gabrielino National Recreation Trail— Chantry Flat to Big Santa Anita Canyon, Newcomb Pass, West Fork of San Gabriel River, Red Box, Arroyo Seco, Altadena

HIKE LENGTH: 28 miles round trip; 4800' elevation gain

CLASSIFICATION: Strenuous (2 days), Moderate (3 or 4 days)

SEASON: November-June

TOPO MAPS: Mt. Wilson, Chilao Flat, Condor Peak, Pasadena

Features

The Gabrielino National Recreation Trail was established by the Forest Service in 1970 as an outgrowth of the National Trails System Act passed by Congress. *This trail has been created for you—the city dweller—so that you might exchange, for a short time, the hectic scene of your urban life for the rugged beauty and freedom of adventure into the solitary wonderland of nature*—so says a Forest Service bulletin announcing the new trail. Actually the trail is not new; it is a joining together and reworking of several old footpaths to form a semicircle over and around the central part of the front range. Enroute you sample the varied terrain and vegetation found in the front range: oak-shaded canyons, spruce- and pine-dotted mountainsides, and chaparral-coated lower slopes. You can camp overnight at any of six Forest Service campgrounds on the circular route.

The name commemorates the Gabrielino Indians, who roamed these mountains long before the advent of the white settlers in Southern

California. These peaceful people migrated into the mountain canyons of the San Gabriels every summer to gather acorns and hunt wild game.

This trip is best done as a 3- or 4-day knapsack venture. If you're in a monumental hurry, you can do it in 2 long days.

Although most of the trail lies within the summer fire-closure area, it is possible to obtain Forest Service permission to do the trip during the closed season *if* the fire danger is not extreme.

Description

Drive to Chantry Flat, 6 miles up Santa Anita Avenue from Arcadia. Arrange to be picked up at the foot of the Arroyo Seco Trail, at the intersection of Ventura Street and Windsor Avenue in Altadena. (The description below is of a 5-day outing. You can vary the trip to suit your own hiking pace and inclination.)

First day: Hike from Chantry Flat up the Big Santa Anita Canyon Trail, passing the first trail camp at Spruce Grove, and continue over Newcomb Pass and down to Devore Trail Camp on the West Fork of the San Gabriel River, 9 miles (see Trip 46). Spend your first night here, or 1 mile farther at the West Fork Public Campground. If you get a late start from Chantry Flat, you can stay the night at Spruce Grove Trail Camp, 4 miles up Big Santa Anita Canyon, adding an extra half day to the trip.

Second day: Hike up the West Fork on the new section of the Gabrielino Trail to Red Box, 6 miles. The easy-graded pathway follows the main creek from DeVore Trail Camp to West Fork Campground, 1 mile, then climbs along the south slope, several hundred feet above the stream, before finally zigzagging up to Red Box saddle. Then you drop into the head of the Arroyo Seco-the trail starts at the northwest edge of the ranger-station parking area—and descend to Commodore Switzer Trail Camp, 4½ miles. This makes 10½ miles for the day. Spend your second night here.

Third day: Descend the Arroyo Seco Trail to Oakwilde (see Trip 16) and on down the canyon to Altadena (see Trip 15), 8½ miles.

If you desire to do the trip in two days, the best overnight camp is Valley Forge Campground, midway up the West Fork. This will give you 12 miles of hiking the first day, and a long 16 the second. Remember, you must camp in one of the authorized campgrounds. ▲

48 Monrovia Canyon Park to Sawpit Canyon, Deer Park

HIKE LENGTH:	6 miles round trip; 1100' elevation gain
CLASSIFICATION:	Moderate
SEASON:	All year
TOPO MAP:	Mt. Wilson, Azusa

Features

Beautiful Sawpit Canyon drains the southern slopes of Monrovia Peak. For fifty years it has been off limits to the public, ostensibly to protect the city of Monrovia's water source. Thanks to a cooperative effort by the city's Community Services Department, the California Conservation Corps and numerous volunteer trail builders, the canyon is once again open to hikers.

This very pleasant trip begins at the lower end of Monrovia Canyon Park, follows the fire road up around Sawpit Canyon Reservoir, and then ascends the new Overturff Trail to a little oak-shaded flat tucked into the south ramparts of Monrovia Peak known as Deer Park. The shady recess was discovered by Monrovia building contractor Ben Overturff about 1905. He built a stone cabin there, and for many years, from 1911 to the 1938 flood, Deer Park Lodge was a popular trail resort. Only the foundations remain today, under a canopy of majestic canyon oaks with a delightful all-year stream nearby.

You must pay a small admission fee—$1 per vehicle on weekdays, $2 on weekends—to enter Monrovia Canyon Park. The Overturff Trail is open every day except Tuesday and Wednesday, when the Monrovia Police Department uses its Sawpit Canyon Shooting Range.

Description

Leave the Foothill Freeway (Interstate 210) at Myrtle Avenue in Monrovia. Drive north on Myrtle, through town, 2 miles to Scenic Drive. Turn right and follow the latter, with short jogs right, then left, curving north as Scenic Drive becomes Canyon Blvd., to Monrovia Canyon Park entrance station. Pay your fee and park in the lower parking area opposite the signed trailhead.

Walk up the Sawpit Canyon fire road, passing Sawpit Dam, built by the Los Angeles County Flood Control District in 1929, and, farther up, Trask Boy Scout Camp, both to your left. The road becomes unpaved just past the dam. After a mile, the road curves left and you reach the lower end of the Overturff Trail on your left, marked by a sign and two low stone pillars.

Follow the trail as it descends to Sawpit Creek, crosses it, and climbs to the Razorback, a sharp divide separating Sycamore and Sawpit canyons. You follow the crest of the Razorback a short distance, then climb the chaparral-covered slope to The Gap, a break in the ridge. Beyond, your pathway descends, contours, and gently climbs beneath a shady canopy of oak and bay laurel. You reach Twin Springs Creek, where flowing water from one of the springs has formed a natural bridge. Just across the creek you pass a junction with a lateral trail that drops down to Sawpit Canyon fire road. You take the main trail straight ahead, climb over a low ridge, cross Deer Park Creek, and reach a second junction. Go left and climb 100 yards to Deer Park. Only the foundations remain of the once-popular lodge, shaded by tall oaks. It's a nice picnic spot.

Return the way you came, or drop down either of the two short lateral trails to Sawpit Canyon fire road and follow the latter back to your car. ▲

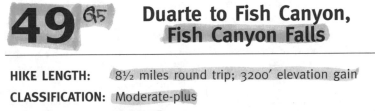

49 ⅌ Duarte to Fish Canyon, Fish Canyon Falls

HIKE LENGTH: 8½ miles round trip; 3200' elevation gain
CLASSIFICATION: Moderate-plus
SEASON: All year
TOPO MAP: Azusa

Features

Fish Canyon Falls are one of the top natural attractions of the San Gabriel Mountains. In spring, when the water runs high, the falls are a spectacular delight, plunging some eighty feet in stairway fashion. The topmost fall is the longest, shooting out from the narrow gorge above, then swishing down into a sparkling pool forty feet below. Then there is a short cascade, followed by a 30-foot plunge into a lower pool, with one final 8-foot drop below that. A fine silver spray dampens the canyon walls when the water runs high, causing them to be embossed with lush green mosses and grasses. In the amphitheater below, a-roar with the boom of the falls, there is a small flat, shaded by oaks and overhanging rock, a favorite spot of picnickers.

For more than a decade, Fish Canyon and its enchanting falls, 2½ miles up from the canyon entrance, were blocked from public access by the quarrying of the Azusa Rock Company. Then, in 1997, the City of Duarte, largely through the efforts of Donna Georgino, was awarded a grant to construct a new trail around the quarry and up to the falls. Work on the new trail was largely done by the California Conservation Corps. The trial was completed and dedicated or public use on June 6, 1998.

The hike into the canyon and on to the falls is no longer the easy walk once was. To avoid the quarry, the new trail climbs 1600' up the west slope of Fish Canyon, then drops 1200' back into the canyon upstream from the quarry. This is an outing recommended for a cool day. Don't try it when the weather is hot; the trail is almost devoid of shade until you approach the falls.

Description

From the Foothill Freeway (I-210) in Duarte, take the Irwindale Avenue off ramp. Drive north to Foothill Blvd. and turn left (west). Follow Foothill, which becomes Huntington Drive, 1 mile to Encanto Parkway. Turn right (north) on the latter, which becomes Fish Canyon Road after 3 blocks, and follow it to a small parking area on the left (west) side of the road about 100 yards short of the quarry entrance. If the parking area is full, park along the road to the south, but *not* alongside the quarry.

The signed trail climbs and switchbacks some 1600 feet up the west slope of Fish Canyon to get around the quarry. It follows the top of a ridge, then, once beyond the quarry, zigzags back down to the old canyon trail above the left (west) bank of the creek.

Once you leave the quarry behind, this becomes a delightful hike. Your trail contours along the west slope about 50 feet above the creek, shaded by a canopy of live oak, big-cone spruce and alder. You pass the foundations of several cabin remains, then switchback higher up the canyon slope before dropping to the creek, 2 miles in. You cross a small tributary stream, then the main creek, and ascend the east slope to a sharp bend in the canyon where the falls abruptly come into view. Carefully descend the rocky slope to a shaded amphitheater alongside a shallow pool, just beneath the falls. Do not attempt to climb the falls, even though the rocks to the left look inviting. People have been severely injured trying.

Return the way you came. Years ago, a trail climbed up the east slope around the falls and continued up Fish Canyon to Stone Cabin Flat, but it has long been abandoned and is now impassable. ▲

50 Mt. Wilson via Kenyon DeVore Trail to West Fork Campground

HIKE LENGTH: 8 miles round trip; 2800' elevation loss and gain.
CLASSIFICATION: Moderate plus
SEASON: All year
TOPO MAP: Mt. Wilson

Features

Kenyon DeVore (1911-1995) spent his whole life in and around the San Gabriel Mountains. He grew up at his parents' trail resorts on the West Fork of the San Gabriel River, first at Camp West Fork, then at Valley Forge Lodge. As a child he busied himself with camp chores. As a teenager he worked at the Mount Wilson Hotel and led a pack train that supplied resorts, forest stations, and campers throughout the mountains. Kenyon spent most of his adult life working for the Los Angeles County Flood Control District, most of the time in San Gabriel Canyon. After his retirement in 1971, he signed on as an Angeles National Forest volunteer, and later as a part-time paid employee. For fifteen years he was a familiar sight at the Chantry Flats visitor information station, giving advice and imparting knowledge to hikers, backpackers, and picnickers. It is only fitting that the old Rattlesnake Trail, which Kenyon traveled many times with his pack train, be renamed in his honor.

The Kenyon DeVore Trail descends Strayns Creek from Mt. Wilson to the West Fork of the San Gabriel. Despite its tortuous and coiling route down the very steep canyon, it is one of the best trail trips in the San Gabriels. Situated entirely on a north-facing slope (the other Mt. Wilson trails approach from the south or the east), the path runs through lush forest all the way-Jeffrey and sugar pine, incense-cedar, big-cone spruce, many stands of oak. Even on a warm day, this well-shaded trip is enjoyable. You cross Strayns Creek several times; in spring and early summer, the trickling water is ice cold and refreshing (but filter it).

Description

Drive up the Angeles Crest Highway to Red Box, 14 miles from La Canada. Turn right and follow Mt. Wilson Road to near the summit, 4 miles. The Kenyon DeVore Trail begins ¼ mile west of the summit, where the pavement splits and becomes one-way. Park in a large clearing south of the road or drive around the loop to a smaller clearing on the north side.

The trail drops north through an oak forest along the west slope of Strayns Canyon. You switchback down through open stands of pine, cross the creek, and contour high along the east slope before switchbacking down to the creek and fording it again to the west slope. Then you descend through a shady pine forest, recross Strayns Creek, and drop to a junction with the Gabrielino Trail, 3 miles. Follow the latter east, along the north slope of the canyon, down to West Fork Campground, 1 mile.

West Fork Campground has stoves, tables and toilets. It is reached by dirt road from Red Box, but as of this writing the road is closed to public autos.

Return the way you came. ▲

51 Mt. Wilson to West Fork Campground, DeVore Trail Camp

HIKE LENGTH:	12 miles round trip; 2900' elevation loss and gain
CLASSIFICATION:	Strenuous (1 Day), Moderate (2 days)
SEASON:	All year
TOPO MAP:	Mt. Wilson

Features

The West Fork of the San Gabriel River—especially the upper part, tucked in behind Mt. Wilson—is a delight to anglers, campers and hikers alike. An all-year stream travels the length of the long canyon, shaded most of the way under oak, bay, maple and spruce. While the canyon has lost some of its primitive charm of yesteryear to the roar of gasoline engines and the screech of brakes, it still offers woodsy haunts and streamside solitude to any who will seek these qualities.

This loop trip, best done as an overnight backpack, drops down from Mt. Wilson and samples the best the West Fork has to offer—the shady streamside stretch between West Fork Campground and DeVore Trail Camp.

Both of these places are rich in history. Adjacent to West Fork Campground, mountain pioneer Louie Newcomb hand-hewed a log cabin in 1900 that was the first ranger station in California and the second in the United States constructed with government funds ($70). Only the foundation remains today; the old ranger station disassembled in 1982 and moved to Chilao, where it has been reassembled as a forestry museum behind the Chilao Visitor Center. Devore Trail Camp stands at the site of old Camp West Fork, a small wilderness resort set up by Ernest and Cherie De Vore in 1913. Camp West Fork was a favorite of anglers, most of whom made the trip in via the Sturtevant Trail from Sierra Madre over Newcomb Pass. It was also popular with hiker as a takeoff point for trips into the backcountry. The camp was abandoned after an ownership dispute in 1925, and now nothing remains of the old hostelry. The Forest Service has made the sylvan site into a trail camp, with stoves and tables and little flats for sleeping.

Make this a two-day trip, staying a night at either West Fork Campground or DeVore Trail Camp, enjoying the gentle murmur of the stream and the soft rustle of leaves in the afternoon breeze. Note: West Fork Campground is reached by dirt road from Red Box, the road is closed indefinitely to public vehicular travel.

Description

Drive to the head of the Kenyon DeVore Trail on Mt. Wilson Road and walk the 4 miles down to West Fork Campground as per Trip 50.

From West Fork Campground cross to the north side of the creek and follow the trail downstream (east) under a forest canopy of oak, alder, maple, bay and big-cone spruce to DeVore Trail Camp, 1 mile. The camp lies on a shady bench on the south side of the creek.

An old anglers' trail continues down the West Fork to Cogswell Reservoir, 5 miles. A few years ago Sierra Club volunteers reworked the first mile of this trail below DeVore Trail Camp. The last 4 miles may some day be reworked, but as of this writing they are overgrown and difficult to follow. Nevertheless, this section of the West Fork contains some of the most beautiful streamside woodland in the San Gabriels. Sample any part of it you can.

To return from DeVore Trail Camp via the recommended loop route, climb steeply south up the Gabrielino Trail, crossing the Red Box-Rincon Fire Road (closed to the public), to Newcomb Pass on the divide between the West Fork and Big Santa Anita watersheds, 3 miles. Then go right (west) and follow the Mt. Wilson Rim Trail, a historic pathway restored by Buddy Nichel and his Boy Scouts, to the summit. Walk through the observatory grounds out the west gate to your car at the Rattlesnake Trail.

Note: The trip should not be made immediately after a heavy rain. The usually serene West Fork can turn into a raging torrent, unsafe to cross. ▲

52 Angeles Crest Highway via Shortcut Canyon to West Fork Campground

HIKE LENGTH:	6 miles round trip; 1800' elevation loss and gain
CLASSIFICATION:	Moderate
SEASON:	All year
TOPO MAPS:	Chilao Flat, Mt. Wilson

Features

Years ago, before the Angeles Crest Highway was a reality, Shortcut Canyon felt the trod of many boots and hooves. Its busy trail, built in 1893 by Louie Newcomb, Arthur Carter and John Hartwell, was the major route into the Charlton Flat-Chilao-Buckhorn backcountry. The canyon and trail were so named because they greatly cut the distance into the mountain interior. The old route was the steep Indian footpath up Valley Forge Canyon and over Barley Flats, now completely disappeared. Today, although the old Shortcut pathway is no longer a major artery of travel, it is part of the Boy Scouts' Silver Moccasin Hike across the range from Red Box to Mt. Baden-Powell (see Appendix I). For this reason, the trail is well-traveled.

This trip now runs from the top down because, as of this writing, the West Fork road from Red Box to West Fork Campground is closed to public autos. Another change is that the historic West Fork Ranger Station, built in 1900 and second-oldest in the nation, has been moved to the Chilao Visitor Center. Still, this is a very pleasant hike. Shortcut

Winter near Chilao

Charles Clark Vernon

Canyon is a woodsy delight, and the West Fork retains its charm of yesteryear. You will get the feel of the old San Gabriels when bandits, hunters, anglers and prospectors rambled into the then-wild heart of the range.

Description

Drive up the Angeles Crest Highway to Shortcut Saddle, 19 miles from La Canada and ¼ mile east of the marked Shortcut Picnic Area. Park in the clearing on the left (north) side of the highway.

From the saddle, take the marked Shortcut Canyon Trail, which leads south. After several short switchbacks you reach a fire road; turn right (west) and follow the fire road about 200 yards, to where you again pick up the trail leading down to your left. You drop steeply down chaparral-coated slopes into the East Fork of Shortcut Canyon. Your path now descends the shady canyon floor and passes the junction of Shortcut's West Fork as you cross and recross the trickling creek. After 3 miles you reach the broad West Fork of the San Gabriel. Boulder-hop across the creek (can be dangerous in times of high water) and reach West Fork Campground, located on a forested bench south of the stream. The campground has stoves, tables and toilets.

From here you have several options. One mile down the West Fork is DeVore Trail Camp (Trip 51). With a car shuttle you can ascend the Kenyon DeVore Trail to Mt. Wilson (Trip 50), or proceed up the Gabrielino Trail to Red Box (Trip 47). Or simply relax a few hours along the sylvan-canopied creek before heading back up Shortcut Canyon to your car. ▲

53   Angeles Forest Highway to Big Tujunga Narrows

HIKE LENGTH: 4 miles round trip; 400' elevation loss and gain
CLASSIFICATION: Moderate
SEASON: All year
TOPO MAP: Condor Peak

Features

Big Tujunga Narrows is one of the more spectacular canyons of the San Gabriel range. Precipitous, rock-ribbed, with turbulent whitewater hurrying through its shaded bowels, it is exceeded in grandeur only by the East Fork of the San Gabriel River. Although hundreds cross the gorge every day via the Angeles Forest Highway's arched bridge, erected in 1941, only a handful venture down into its cavernous depths. This trip takes you through the heart of the Narrows, first via an exceedingly steep footpath, then by boulder-hopping alongside the tumultuous stream. Although you're right below a well-traveled highway, the scene is as wild as you can find in the Angeles. One word of warning: Don't attempt this trip immediately after heavy rains; Big Tujunga turns into a raging torrent and has claimed several lives in recent years.

Description

Drive up the Angeles Crest Highway to Clear Creek Junction, then left on the Angeles Forest Highway (L.A. County Road N3). to an unmarked parking area shaded by a lone incense-cedar on your right, 15½ miles from La Canada. If you reach the Narrows Bridge, you've driven ⅓ mile too far.

Cross the highway and follow an unmarked trail steeply down the slope. Halfway down, the trail divides into several very steep paths. Take extreme care as you descend the last hundred feet to the canyon floor. Please *do not* climb down over the concrete gauging station. Here, in the middle of Big Tujunga Narrows, you have a choice.

If you decide to venture upstream, the first ¾ mile is easy going, as you pass the confluence of Mill Creek and walk under the spectacular Narrows Bridge, looming far above, a marvel of steel and concrete. Beyond the bridge, Big Tujunga twists and turns in an easterly direction, and you must scramble over and around jumbo streamside boulders. Notice the chaparral on the sun-drenched south-facing slope and big-cone spruce on the shady north-facing slope—very characteristic of canyons in the San Gabriels. In ¾ mile you reach a waterfall. This is as far as you can safely go, so return the same way.

If you choose to explore downstream from the Flood Control District gaging station, the going is more difficult. In ¼ mile you reach the granite-enclosed gorge of the lower Narrows and its foot-wetting fords. It is 1½ rough miles down to Forest Road 3N27, through an area of cascades and small waterfalls. This traverse is for experienced cross-country hikers only, and *never* should be attempted during times of high water.

(*Note:* This trip replaces the Monte Cristo Mine hike in previous editions of this guidebook. The owners of the Monte Cristo have closed their property to visitors.) ▲

54 Mt. Gleason Road to Mt. Gleason

HIKE LENGTH:	5 miles round trip; 1000′ elevation gain
CLASSIFICATION:	Moderate
SEASON:	May-October
TOPO MAP:	Acton

Features

The long, forested hogback of Mt. Gleason (6502′) dominates the western end of the San Gabriels. From Gleason's broad summit you look north across the drab expanse of the Mojave Desert and, on the dearest of days, you can just make out, far on the distant horizon, the angular snow-streaked peaks of the southern High Sierra.

The mountain is drenched in history. In 1869 George Gleason, first postmaster of Ravenna and superintendent of the rich Eureka Mine near present-day Acton, climbed the north slope in quest of the timber stands he saw on top. Instead, he found gold. Men swarmed up the mountain, and the Mount Gleason Mining District was organized. Transporting the gold-bearing quartz down the steep slopes to the mill in Soledad Canyon was a harrowing process. Logs were fastened behind the ore-filled wagons, pulled by eight-mule teams, to slow the descent. Even so, accidents occurred with regularity. The most active period for the Gleason Mines was from 1888 to 1896, when some twenty prospects were being worked and a five-stamp mill was erected high on the north slope. The richest mines were named the Gleason, the Lost Padres and the Eagle. There has been limited activity into recent years, but only the miners' ghosts remain now.

This is a delightful stroll through forest and chaparral, on trail all the way, with far-ranging desert views. If you're experienced in cross-country travel and don't mind some bushwhacking, you can drop down Gleason's north slope and visit the old mining district.

Description

Drive up the Angeles Crest Highway to Clear Creek Junction, then left on the Angeles Forest Highway (L.A. County Road N3) to Mill Creek Summit, 23 miles from La Canada. Turn left (west) and follow the Mt. Gleason Road (signed MESSENGER FLATS 12), passing a Pacific Crest Trail junction in 2½ miles (you can start your hike here if you don't mind adding 8 miles round trip to it), to a road junction in 6 miles, just outside the Youth Conservation Camp. Drive left and continue on Mount Gleason Road ½ mile to where it bottoms out. Park in the clearing to your right.

Walk right to the lower, east end of the clearing, where you will see a yellow locked gate and a poor dirt road descending northward. Pass the gate and walk down the road only about 25 yards to where you intersect the Pacific Crest Trail. Go left and follow the PCT as it climbs west, then northwest, under a canopy of interior live oak, black oak, big-cone spruce and incense cedar. As you climb higher on the north shoulder of Mount Gleason, Jeffrey pines become predominant and views open northward over the shimmering Mojave Desert. You cross an old dirt road and, ¼ mile farther, make a sharp switchback up to the top of Mt. Gleason's west ridge. Leave the PCT here and go left (east) over several hummocks to the top. The large concrete structure you see here is the foundation of a disassembled Air Force radar dome.

Return the way you came. If you are an experienced mountaineer and wish to see what remains of the old gold mines, leave the PCT at the before-mentioned switchback and drop north, a gentle descent at first that becomes increasingly steeper. After descending about 600 feet, veer left into Gleason Canyon's west fork, where you will pick up a steep old mining road. Evidence of past diggings is all around you. The major mines are to your left, on the opposite slope, guarded by thick chaparral that makes them difficult to reach. Continue on the old road, mostly down but with several short uphill pitches, to the floor of the main canyon, then steeply up to your car. This option adds 2 miles to the trip. ▲

55   Charlton Flat to Vetter Mountain Lookout

HIKE LENGTH: 2 miles round trip; 400' elevation gain

CLASSIFICATION: Easy

SEASON: All year

TOPO MAP: Chilao Flat

Features

Simply put, Vetter Mountain offers you maximum view for minimum effort. The fire lookout, perched on this prominent high point above Charlton Flat, affords a rewarding 360-degree panorama of the heartland of the San Gabriels. To the south, the dark summits of the front range, dominated by Strawberry and San Gabriel peaks, rise above smog-assaulted slopes. Eastward lies the rugged depression of the San Gabriel Wilderness, and the gray mass of Old Baldy looms on the distant skyline. To the north, beyond the pine flats of Charlton and Chilao, rise the backbone peaks of the range—Pacifico, Waterman, Twin Peaks, Williamson. Westward and southwestward, the ridgeline drops steeply into the trenches of Alder Creek and the Big Tujunga. All of this view is yours for a half-hour's effort.

The Vetter Mountain Lookout is no longer in use. The old lookout building has been restored and re-equipped to serve as a visitor information center.

Description

Drive up the Angeles Crest Highway to Charlton Flat, 24 miles from La Canada. Turn left into the Charlton Flat Picnic Area; follow the upper road (far left) to the locked gate at the beginning of the Vetter Lookout access road. Park here, taking care not to block the road.

Walk up the dirt access road, traveling west with a switchback near the end, to the summit fire lookout.

An alternate route, slightly longer and with 200' more gain, begins near the northwest, lower end of the picnic area, across from the Wolf Tree Nature Trail. A wooden sign saying VETTER MTN. points the way. The trail follows a shallow draw southwestward, crossing two fire roads at midpoint, to the summit ridge just west of the lookout. From the ridge, turn left and climb 200 yards to the top. ▲

56 Mill Creek Summit to Mt. Pacifico Campground

HIKE LENGTH:	6 miles one way; 2200' elevation gain
CLASSIFICATION:	Moderate
SEASON:	May-October
TOPO MAP:	Pacifico Mountain

Features

7124-foot Pacifico Mountain looms high on the northern rampart of the San Gabriels, offering far-reaching panoramas over Antelope Valley and the Mojave Desert. On days when the sky is clear of the usual desert haze, the viewer can make out, on the distant horizon, the sawtooth peaks of the High Sierra and the distinct cone-shaped summit of Telescope Peak overlooking Death Valley.

Legend says that Pacifico Mountain and its all-year spring were a hangout of Tiburcio Vasquez and his gang of horse thieves in the 1870s. In fact, the infamous *bandido* supposedly gave it the name "Pacifico" because he could see the Pacific Ocean from the top.

This very pleasant, view-rich trip follows the easy-graded Pacific Crest Trail most of the way, then climbs to the Mt. Pacifico Campground, right on the summit, via the campground road or the west ridge. If you reverse the trip, it's all downhill. A car shuttle is recommended.

Description

Drive up the Angeles Crest Highway to Clear Creek Junction, then left on the Angeles Forest Highway (L.A. County Road N3) to Mill Creek Summit, 23 miles from La Canada. Drive another car to, or arrange to be picked up at, Mt. Pacifico Campground. To reach the latter from Mill Creek Summit, turn right (east) and follow Forest Road 3N17 to the summit campground, 6 miles.

From the Mill Creek Summit parking area, cross Forest Road 3N17 to the signed Pacific Crest Trail heading northeast. The trail climbs, then contours just below and behind the Forest Service maintenance station. Beyond, the pathway gently climbs eastward, then northward, through an open forest of bigcone spruce and interior live oak, around the head of Tie Canyon. You ascend chaparral-clad slopes to a ridge-crest, where expansive views open northward across Antelope Valley and the Mojave Desert. Then you round the ridge and turn south, intersecting an old, abandoned dirt road. Your trail follows the roadbed ½ mile, turns left and ascends eastward, then southeast, under a cool canopy of oaks and Jeffrey pines. You reach a forested gap and a junction with the Mt. Pacifico Campground road in 5 miles. The Pacific Crest Trail, which you have been following, turns north, but you leave it here and have a choice of routes. You can follow the gently graded

Jumbo boulders and Jeffrey pines on Pacifico Mountain

campground road to the summit, 1¼ miles, or climb the shorter but steeper west ridge to the top.

For a much easier trip, reverse it. Leave the Mt. Pacifico Campground road where it intersects the PCT, ¼ mile up from Forest Road 3N17, and walk downhill all the way to Mill Creek Summit. ▲

57   Chilao to Devils Canyon, San Gabriel Wilderness

HIKE LENGTH:	7 miles round trip; 1500' elevation loss and gain
CLASSIFICATION:	Moderate
SEASON:	November-April
TOPO MAPS:	Chilao Flat, Waterman Mountain

Features

Less than 20 air miles from downtown Los Angeles is the San Gabriel Wilderness, 36,000 acres of rugged ridge and canyon country forever protected and preserved in its natural state. No roads here, no resorts, no noisy public campgrounds; only the primeval sounds of earth—the wind rustling leaves of pine and alder, the stream dancing over boulder and cascade, the wrentit's staccato call, on rare occasions the mountain lion darting through brush. Only three maintained trails enter this wilderness. The one perhaps most delightful leaves the Angeles Crest at Chilao and descends steep slopes of chaparral, spruce, and pine into the shaded bowels of Devils Canyon. Here, under a green canopy of alder and willow, alongside deep pools and miniature waterfalls, the hiker can find solitude on a day's outing or overnight knapsack, and relive a part of the mountains as they once were.

Take care; this is an upside-down trip—downhill all the way in, uphill on the return. Many an out-of-condition rambler has strided gaily down, only to labor painfully every upward step out.

Description

A prominent sign marks the Devils Canyon trailhead on the Angeles Crest Highway, 27 miles from La Canada and about 200 yards *before* you reach the Chilao Visitor Center turnoff. Leave your car in the large parking area on the left (west) side of the road, directly across from the trailhead.

The trail, well-maintained by the Forest Service, is easy to follow. It loses no time in descending the steep hillsides, alternately through stands of big-cone spruce on shady north faces and dense chaparral on sunnier slopes. About halfway down the trail meets a small tributary creek and then follows it to the main canyon. At its end, on a shaded bench on your right, well above the stream, is a wilderness camping area.

It is possible, without inordinate difficulty for the average hiker, to follow Devils Canyon downstream about 2 miles—crossing and recrossing the creek, boulder-hopping, and occasionally thrashing through willow and brush. Beyond this, the canyon narrows, sidewalls steepen, and waterfalls assume grander proportions: this is experts' country, only for the experienced climber with rope and climbing hardware.

Allow plenty of time for the return trip—at least twice what it took to get in. Remember, it's all uphill. ▲

Devils Canyon, San Gabriel Wilderness

58 Chilao to Horse Flats, Mt. Hillyer

HIKE LENGTH:	6 miles round trip; 1000' elevation gain
CLASSIFICATION:	Moderate
SEASON:	All year
TOPO MAP:	Chilao Flat

Features

The Chilao-Horse Flats country is a gentle region of rounded ridgetops, shallow draws, and small flats set deep in the heart of the San Gabriels. The forest here is open and parklike; tail Jeffrey pines and incense cedars cluster in sheltered recesses and dot the rolling hillsides. The chaparral is rich and green and the sky a deep blue, with seldom a trace of the brown murkiness that so often invades the south slope of the range. It is ideal picnicking, camping and hiking country.

A century ago this was *bandido* country. The notorious Tiburcio Vasquez and his gang of horse thieves utilized Chilao and Horse Flats—then deep in the wilderness and little-known—as refuges from the law, as hideouts where they could rest and plan their next raid, and as pastures for stolen horses. The great boulders of nearby Mt. Hillyer furnished an impregnable fortress if pursuing posses came too close. One of Vasquez's men at Chilao was a herder named Jose Gonzales, noted among his cohorts for his skill with a knife. On one occasion he killed a bear with some slick knife-work, earning the nickname "Chillia" (hot stuff). From this allegedly came the name *Chilao*.

There are no *bandidos* here now, and roads lace the region, but the country still holds appeal. This very pleasant trail hike takes you through the best of the Chilao-Horse Flats area, and climbs through magnificent stands of Jeffrey pine and around jumbo boulders to the summit of Mt. Hillyer.

Description

Drive up the Angeles Crest Highway to the turnoff for the Chilao Visitor Center, 27 miles from La Canada. Turn left and drive down the paved road, passing the visitor center, ½ mile to a clearing on your right, where a sign indicates SILVER MOCCASIN TRAIL. Park here.

Proceed up the trail as it switchbacks through chaparral and clusters of Jeffrey pine to a junction just short of Horse Flats Campground, 1 mile. Turn left, leaving the Silver Moccasin Trail, and follow the path 100 yards to the south edge of the campground. A sign to your left indicates MT. HILLYER, 2 MILES. Proceed up the Mt. Hillyer Trail through open clusters of manzanita, scrub oak and Jeffrey pine, around a maze of giant granite boulders, to the broad summit of Mt. Hillyer. You can't see much from the forested top, but if you walk several hundred feet southwest onto the fire break, you are rewarded with a fine panorama of the rolling bandido country to the south and southeast, and the broad trench of Alder Creek dropping off to the west.

Return the same way. A very pleasant option, adding 2 miles to the round trip, is to go north from the summit along the ridgetop trail, which climbs gently over two nubbins before descending to a junction with the Santa Clara Divide Road (3N17). Turn right (southeast) and follow the paved road, then right again on the Horse Flats Campground access road to Horse Flats, where you meet your trail of ascent. From here, follow the same route down to your car.

A very easy way to climb Mt. Hillyer is from the Santa Clara Divide Road (3N17) mentioned above.

Drive the Angeles Crest Highway to its junction with the Santa Clara Divide Road, indicated by a metal sign, 29½ miles from La Canada and 2½ miles past Chilao. Turn left (west) and follow the paved road past the entrance to Horse Flats Campground to a saddle where the road crosses a crest, 3 miles from the highway and 0.3 mile beyond the campground entrance. Park in the parking area to your left.

Walk south along the divide (once a dirt road), then up the broad fuel break, over several nubbins to the unmarked summit, 1¼ miles.

You can cut 2 miles off the round trip by driving to Horse Flats Campground. turn left off Angeles Crest Highway 2½ miles north of Chilao, where a sign indicates SANTA CLARA DIVIDE ROAD, and proceed 2½ miles on this road to the campground. ▲

59 Three Points to Twin Peaks Saddle, Twin Peaks, Mt. Waterman, and Buckhorn

HIKE LENGTH: 14 miles (total); 3700' elevation gain

CLASSIFICATION: Strenuous

SEASON: June-October

TOPO MAP: Waterman Mountain

Features

This trip traverses the high country along the northern boundary of the San Gabriel Wilderness and climbs the two major peaks in the region. From the ramparts of Mt. Waterman and Twin Peaks (especially the latter), you look down over the extremely rugged upper reaches of Devils and Bear canyons, the wildest mountain country in the San Gabriels. Here, among the crags and in the deep recesses, is the undisturbed lair of mountain lion, black bear, and bighorn sheep, animals seldom seen in the more frequented parts of the range.

This is delightful wilderness country. The topography is more broken than in most other parts of the range, and jumbo boulders dot the slopes. The chaparral is tall and richly textured. The forest, primarily Jeffrey and ponderosa pine, is open and parklike, carpeted with pine needles. Over near Twin Peaks Saddle are some of the most beautiful stands of incense cedar in the range. On sunny slopes, lupines stand bright and pagodalike in early summer. Half a dozen trickling rills line the route during early season, only to disappear one by one as the dry months progress.

A car shuttle between Three Points and Buckhorn is required if you wish to do the full traverse. Although the total trip is classified as strenuous, parts of it can be taken and thoroughly enjoyed by the neophyte. A 2-mile stroll up-trail from Three Points will reward the beginner with superb vistas into Devils Canyon. If you are a hiker of moderate ability, you can continue 4 more miles to Twin Peaks Saddle and return. This high wilderness is really too good to be reserved for only the strongest; it is there for all.

Description

Drive the Angeles Crest Highway to Three Points Junction, 2.4 miles beyond (north of) Chilao. Three Points is indicated on the map, but there is no such sign on the highway; look for the junction of the side road to Horse Flats (wooden sign). One car must be shuttled 5 miles farther to Buckhorn, to be used on the return trip.

The trail, 100 feet west of the Horse Flats Road turnoff, is marked by a large wooden sign indicating, among other things, MT. WATERMAN, 7 MILES. It leads south from the highway, passes two junctions (left first, then right—follow MT. WATERMAN signs), and starts zigzagging up the west spine of the mountain. After gaining about 600' the route levels off and traverses around the long, indented slopes of Waterman. The deep trench of Devils Canyon is constantly in view to your right. Keep a sharp lookout for bighorn sheep; they are occasionally seen here. The trail rounds the mountain and after 5 miles reaches a junction—left up to Mt. Waterman, right down to Twin Peaks Saddle. Go right, follow the trail 1 mile, descending 400', to Twin Peaks Saddle. Here the maintained trail ends, but a pathway worn by climbers, very steep in places, leads up the north slope of Twin Peaks 1200' to the summit (the eastern of the two peaks is higher). This is the climax of the trip; from the top you see nature's pattern of the entire San Gabriel Wilderness, a panorama you have nowhere else.

Return to Twin Peaks Saddle, then walk up-trail 1 mile to the afore-mentioned junction. This time take the right fork and climb 1200' more (2 miles) to the summit of Mt. Waterman, the highest point in the wilderness area. After taking in the view (excellent, but not as good as from Twin Peaks), descend the main trail to Buckhorn (see Trip 60). ▲

60 Buckhorn to Mt. Waterman

HIKE LENGTH:	6 miles round trip; 1300' elevation gain
CLASSIFICATION:	Moderate
SEASON:	June-October
TOPO MAP:	Waterman Mountain

Features

In 1889, when the San Gabriels were almost totally wild and unex-plored, and grizzly-infested, Bob Waterman, his bride Liz, and Commodore Ferry Switzer, all of famed Switzer's Camp in the Arroyo Seco, made a three-week trip across the range to the desert and back. Enroute they scrambled up the highest mountain in the vicinity to get

On the Waterman Trail

their bearings. On the summit they built a cairn and left a register. In honor of Liz, who they believed to be the first white woman to cross the range, the two men christened the peak "Lady Waterman Mountain." Years later, when the USGS mapped the mountain, they left off the "Lady" part of the designation. Bob Waterman, who lived many years longer in Pasadena, tried several times to restore his wife's honor by putting the "Lady" back on the peak, but to no avail. Today, it's just "Mt. Waterman."

8038' Mt. Waterman is best known to skiers. Several ski lifts ascend the broad north slope of the mountain, making it one of the most popular winter sports areas in the range. But in summer, when the snow is gone, Mt. Waterman becomes the sole domain of the hiker. Most climbers take this well-graded, easy-to-follow trail from Buckhorn, the shortest way up the mountain (unless you ride the ski lift).

Waterman is an elongated, broad-summited mountain, shaped like a mammoth "U," with three high points. The highest of the high points lies near the southwestern edge of the summit plateau. From here, you are rewarded with a panoramic vista of the entire western San Gabriels, with particularly fine views into the depths of Devils Canyon.

Description

Drive the Angeles Crest Highway to Buckhorn Ranger Station, 34 miles from La Canada. Park on one of the wide shoulders alongside the highway.

The trailhead here is confusing because of a profusion of fire roads and footpaths that climb the north slope of Mt. Waterman from the highway. The correct trail is the one farthest to the left (east). At the MT. WATERMAN TRAIL sign walk about 30 feet up the fire road, then go left on a section of trail which parallels the highway for a short distance, crosses another fire road, and begins to ascend the forested slope. After climbing southward through tall stands of Jeffrey pine and incense cedar for 1¼ miles, the trail reaches a saddle on Waterman's east ridge; from here you look down into the wild upper reaches of Bear Canyon and to Twin Peaks beyond. The trail now turns west and climbs to a junction with the Twin Peaks Trail, ½ mile. Go right and continue up to the broad, undulating summit plateau. The trail does not reach the actual summit of Waterman; when it turns northwest and begins to descend, leave the trail and head southwest, past a subsidiary summit, about 500 yards to the true summit. ▲

61

Cloudburst Summit to Cooper Canyon, Cooper Canyon Trail Camp, Buckhorn Campground

HIKE LENGTH: 6 miles round trip; 1300' elevation loss, 800' gain

CLASSIFICATION: Moderate

SEASON: May-October

TOPO MAP: Waterman Mountain

Features

Beautiful, woodsy Cooper Canyon, a major tributary of Little Rock Creek, has long been a favorite of hikers. Its little singing creek, shaded by beautiful stands of Jeffrey and sugar pine, cedar, alder and oak, was once a favorite Indian haunt. According to mountain historian Will Thrall, braves camped at Buckhorn, just over the ridge, and sent their squaws and papooses here while the men hunted and raised a ruckus. For many years the old Indian campsite in the upper canyon-now Cooper Canyon Trail Camp—was known as Squaw Camp. The canyon became the favorite hunting ground of Pasadena brothers Ike and Tom Cooper during the '90s, when deer and bear were plentiful. The Cooper brothers are long gone, but their exploits are eternalized by the canyon name.

This loop trip, requiring a car shuttle between Cloudburst Summit on the Angeles Crest Highway and Buckhorn Campground, takes you down through this richly forested recess where nature's stillness reigns supreme. To make the trip more leisurely and allow time to enjoy the beauty of this canyon country, stay overnight at Cooper Canyon Trail Camp.

Description

Drive up the Angeles Crest Highway to Cloudburst Summit, 33 miles from La Canada. Park in the clearing to the left (north) of the highway, where the fire road descends into Cooper Canyon, taking care not to block the dirt roadway. The trip will finish at Buckhorn Campground, 1½ miles east, just off the highway. Either have a car waiting there or plan to walk back up the highway to Cloudburst Summit.

Proceed past the locked gate and 1¾ miles down the fire road to Cooper Canyon Trail Camp, on a forested bench to your right. Tables, stoves and toilet make this a convenient overnight camp spot. Then take the broad trail (once a road) down Cooper Canyon 1¼ miles to its junction with the Burkhart Trail leading up to Buckhorn. Turn right and follow the latter 1¾ miles up to Buckhorn Campground hiker's parking area (see Trip 62). ▲

62 Buckhorn Campground to Cooper Canyon, Little Rock Creek

HIKE LENGTH:	5 miles round trip; 900' elevation loss and gain
CLASSIFICATION:	Moderate
SEASON:	May-October
TOPO MAP:	Waterman Mountain

Features

Nestled in deep canyons north of Mt. Waterman and Kratka Ridge are woodsy hideaways where nature, at her quiet, pristine best, still reigns relatively undisturbed by the markings of man. Buckhorn Canyon, Cooper Canyon and upper Little Rock Creek are three of the most delightful sylvan recesses in Angeles National Forest. Sparkling streams glide and dance and tumble over boulders, and cascade down miniature waterfalls, shaded by a magnificent forest of Jeffrey and sugar pine, incense cedar, alder and oak. Ferns and lush grasses sprout emerald-green along the banks and, in spring and early summer, mountain wildflowers add a dash of color.

This trip—one of the best in the San Gabriels—takes you from Buckhorn Public Campground down along the slopes of Buckhorn Canyon into shady Cooper Canyon and on to Little Rock Creek. Anglers as well as nature lovers will enjoy the jaunt, for there are rainbow trout in Little Rock Creek.

Pine- and cedar-shaded Buckhorn was once an Indian haunt, back when Shoshonean peoples frequented the range in search of scorns, pine nuts and wild game. You can still find large boulders with mortar holes worn into them, used by Indians to grind meal. After the Indian came the white hunter. Buckhorn was a back-country hangout for hunters, seeking the abundant wild game. The name "Buckhorn" dates from this period—a pair of king-sized buck horns were once nailed to a tree here. Today Buckhorn is a well-equipped public campground, one of the favorites of Angeles Forest campers.

Description

Drive up the Angeles Crest Highway to Buckhorn Campground, 34 miles from La Canada and ½ mile past the Mt. Waterman Ski Area.

Turn left and follow the Buckhorn Campground Road through the campground to the hikers' parking area just beyond. (Do not park in the campground proper.)

Take the Burkhart Trail from the north end of the parking area down-canyon along the left (northeast) slope. Follow this trail as it descends through pine and cedar into Cooper Canyon, where you intersect the Cooper Canyon Trail (see Trip 61), 1¾ miles. Take the right fork and follow the trail ¼ mile down Cooper Canyon, through a wilderness garden of green around small Cooper Canyon Falls, to Little Rock Creek. Here your Burkhart Trail intersects the Rattlesnake Trail leading east up Little Rock Creek to the Angeles Crest Highway (see Trip 64).

There is no trail down Little Rock Creek; however, you can explore the canyon quite a distance by boulder-hopping. Take care if it's spring and the snowpack on the higher mountains is melting; Little Rock Creek runs high then.

Return the way you came—all uphill now. ▲

63 Buckhorn to Little Rock Creek, Burkhart Saddle, Pleasant View Ridge

HIKE LENGTH: 14 miles round trip; 3300' elevation gain
CLASSIFICATION: Strenuous
SEASON: May-October
TOPO MAPS: Waterman Mountain, Juniper Hills

Features

Long, sinuous Pleasant View Ridge lives up to its name. The hiker resting in the shade of tall Jeffrey pines on its crest can gaze far out into the seemingly endless Mojave Desert. On the dearest of days, you can make out the tawny, sharp-toothed ramparts of the southern Sierra Nevada, over 60 miles distant.

Looking at Pleasant View Ridge from the Angeles Crest Highway, you may think it close at hand. But it's farther than you realize. Separating the ridge from the main body of the range is the V-shaped trench of Little Rock Creek, a desert-bound creek whose canyon holds sylvan surprises where you might least expect to find them. To reach Pleasant View, you must descend into the deep canyon and climb up the other side.

Be in shape for this one. It's up and down both ways, with little level going. If the day's warm, carry two canteens.

Description

Drive up the Angeles Crest Highway to the Buckhorn Campground hikers' parking area (see Trip 62), 34 miles from La Canada.

Walk down the rear access road into the campground and turn right. Follow the trail that leaves from near the east end of the campground and descends to Little Rock Creek, 2 miles (see Trip 62 for trail description). Here you intersect the Rattlesnake Trail coming down from Eagles Roost Picnic Area (see Trip 64). Take the left fork and follow the Burkhart Trail as it steadily climbs around a ridge, crosses a small creek (water in spring and early summer) and zigzags 3½ miles up 1300' to Burkhart Saddle.

Here you have three options.

You can enjoy the desert view from here and return the way you came.

You can turn left (west) and follow an unmarked trail up around the slopes of Will Thrall Peak to a pleasant, Jeffrey-forested bench just west of the high point, then scramble up to the 7983' summit of Pleasant View Ridge, slightly more than a mile, with 1000' elevation gain, from the saddle. From here the view is really outstanding.

You can descend the desert side of the Burkhart Trail to Devils Punchbowl (see Trip 67), if you can arrange a very long car shuttle.

Whichever option you take, you are certain to enjoy this northern extremity of the San Gabriels, where the aroma of desert sage blends with the sweet scent of mountain pine and cedar. ▲

64 Eagles Roost Picnic Area to Little Rock Creek

HIKE LENGTH: 6 miles round trip; 1100' elevation loss and gain

CLASSIFICATION: Moderate

SEASON: May-October

TOPO MAP: Waterman Mountain

Features

Some of the most magnificent canyon country in the San Gabriel Mountains lies on the desert slopes of the range. Nowhere is this more evident than in the uppermost reaches of Little Rock Creek, close under

Kratka Ridge and Mt. Williamson's southwest shoulder. The terrain is rugged and colorful—sheer crags of whitish rock stand in stark contrast to wrinkled slopes of reddish-brown and gray. Jeffrey, sugar and Coulter pines, white firs, incense cedars, and oaks crowd canyon recesses and dot open ridges. The delightful stream, fed by springs high in the granite folds of Mt. Williamson, runs all year.

This trip leaves the Angeles Crest Highway opposite Eagles Roost Picnic Area and descends the old Rattlesnake Trail (not as ominous as it sounds) into the upper reaches of Little Rock Creek. Once you leave the highway, you drop into recesses as magnificently wild as any in the range. If you like primitive canyon country relatively undisturbed by the presence of man, this hike should be a rewarding experience.

Description

Drive up the Angeles Crest Highway to Eagles Roost Picnic Area, just before you reach a brown highway-maintenance shed, 39 miles from La Canada. Park in the clearing.

Cross the highway and descend west on the unmarked fire road into the head of Little Rock Creek. After ½ mile the fire road narrows into a regular trail, and then continues dropping to the canyon bottom, ½ mile farther. Here, amid a darkened forest, alongside the cold waters of the creek, you will be tempted to pause. A 200-yard side trip upstream brings you to a sparkling pool beneath a miniature waterfall. Back on the main route, follow the trail as it contours along the north slope of the gorge, heading downstream (west). For the next two miles, you round rocky points, with the creek far below, and pass through sheltered recesses. Finally you drop down alongside the creek and reach a junction with the Burkhart Trail.

Here you have several options. You can return up the Rattlesnake Trail, the way you came. You can turn left (southwest) and ascend the trail to Buckhorn Campground (see Trip 62). This makes a very pleasant circle trip and requires a 4-mile car shuttle between Eagles Roost and Buckhorn. Or you can turn right (north) and ascend the Burkhart trail to Pleasant View Ridge (see Trip 63), then return.

Experienced hikers have descended trailless Little Rock Creek from the Burkhart Trail all the way to the lower Little Rock Creek Road, 8 boulder-hopping miles. Two warnings if you want to try this: don't do it alone; and don't do it when the stream is high. ▲

65

Mt. Williamson from Angeles Crest Highway

HIKE LENGTH: 5 miles round trip; 1600' elevation gain
CLASSIFICATION: Moderate
SEASON: June-October
TOPO MAP: Crystal Lake

Features

8214-foot Mt. Williamson stands tall and massive, jutting northward from the main crest of the range like a bold sentinel guarding the green high country from the withering influence of the desert 5000' below. It is buttressed on the south by formidable cliffs, through which the Angeles Crest Highway tunnels, and on the north it plunges abruptly down to that fantastic jumble of whitish rocks known as the Devils Punchbowl.

The mountain is named for Lieutenant Robert Stockton Williamson of the U.S. Army, who led a reconnaissance of the north slopes of the San Gabriels for the Pacific Railroad Survey in 1853. He was looking for a railway route across the mountains. (Williamson didn't fail. He located *two* railway routes across the mountains—Soledad Pass and Cajon Pass.) The report he submitted to Congress contained the first detailed description of the desert side of the range.

From the summit of Mt. Williamson, you get an eagle's eye view of the broken country explored by this army officer more than a century ago. It has changed much, but the strange geological features—the scarps, bee-line valleys, troughs, sag ponds, and most of all the twisted and folded rocks of the Devil's Punchbowl—are the same. Mt. Williamson towers directly above the San Andreas Rift Zone, the most monumental earthquake fault in the United States. Its unique pattern is readily observable to any who walk a short distance north from the summit and look down. The fault line can be seen extending along the entire northern base of the San Gabriels, from northwest to southeast. Only from Mt. Williamson or from high points along Pleasant View Ridge immediately to the northwest do you get this perspective.

Description

You can start up Mt. Williamson from either of two points along the Angeles Crest Highway, roughly 40 miles from La Canada. One is an unnamed saddle 2.4 miles east of the Kratka Ridge ski area, ¼ mile west of the tunnels; the other is Islip Saddle, 1.6 miles farther east. From both places trails ascend to the south ridge of Williamson. If you can arrange a car shuttle, go up one way and down the other.

From the unnamed, unsigned saddle beyond Kratka Ridge, follow the dirt road uphill 100 yards, then turn right onto the trail that switchbacks up Williamson's southwest ridge. You pass through an open forest of Jeffrey and ponderosa pine, with white fir becoming more abundant as you near 8000'. In about 2 miles you reach the ridgetop and meet the trail coming up from Islip Saddle. From this point you are rewarded with a superb view southward, directly into the rugged trench of Bear Canyon, 3000' below. To reach the summit, follow a faint trail northward along the ridge, climbing over several bumps to the 8214' high point overlooking the desert. This point is shown as the summit on the Topo map, although a bump ¼ mile north-

High on Mt. Williamson Ridge   Betty Dessert

west is 30′ higher and offers a better view of the Devils Punchbowl country.

If you start from Islip Saddle, take the trail that leads northwest up the ridge. After slightly less than 2 miles of steady climbing, you reach the ridgetop and meet the above-described trail coming up from the west. ▲

66 Angeles Crest Highway to Mt. Williamson, Pleasant View Ridge, Burkhart Saddle, Little Rock Creek, Eagles Roost

HIKE LENGTH: 12 miles round trip; 3500′ elevation gain

CLASSIFICATION: Strenuous

SEASON: June-October

TOPO MAPS: Crystal Lake, Valyermo, Juniper Hills, Waterman Mountain

Features

This is a long up-and-down ramble over the northern crest of the San Gabriels, partly on trail, partly cross country. The trip features a trailless traverse along the rim of Pleasant View Ridge between Mt. Williamson and Burkhart Saddle, with continuous views over desert and high mountain country. It is a tough but rewarding experience for those in top physical condition. Don't try it alone; much of the terrain covered is seldom trod by human foot and rescue would be difficult. Carry two full canteens; most of the route is waterless.

Description

Drive up the Angeles Crest Highway to the beginning of the Mt. Williamson west trail, 39 miles from La Canada and 2½ miles beyond the Kratka Ridge ski area (see Trip 65).

Take the trail to the summit of Mt. Williamson (see Trip 65). Leave the trail at the summit and walk northwest along the top of Pleasant View Ridge, repeatedly losing and gaining several hundred feet of elevation, for 3 miles to Burkhart Saddle. This cross-country jaunt is open, through a rich forest of Jeffrey pine, but the steep up and down is tiring. Rest often and enjoy the superb desert view, with occasional glimpses down into the heart of the Devils Punchbowl. From Burkhart

Saddle, turn left (south) and follow the Burkhart Trail down to Little Rock Creek (see Trip 63). From the creek, pick up the Rattlesnake Trail and follow it east, along the north slope of the canyon, up to the Angeles Crest Highway opposite Eagles Roost Picnic Area (see Trip 64). Walk northeast on the highway ½ mile to your car. ▲

67 Burkhart Trail—Devils Punchbowl to Pleasant View Ridge

HIKE LENGTH:	10 miles round trip; 2300′ elevation gain
CLASSIFICATION:	Moderate
SEASON:	October-June
TOPO MAP:	Juniper Hills

Features

South from Littlerock and Pearblossom, a number of rounded ridgelines rise rather abruptly from the desert. Most prominent of these is Pleasant View Ridge, a long, sinuous hogback that begins its upward trend near Juniper Hills, leads southeasterly, and reaches its climax on 8214′ Mt. Williamson. The ridge is aptly named. The hiker resting atop

Devils Punchbowl   Will Thrall

one of its many welts can look down upon little valleys and low foothills resplendent with the Mojave's best-known symbol—the beautiful joshua tree, sharing the landscape with clusters of mesquite, purple sage and yucca. In springtime, after abundant rain, the foothills are carpeted with colorful wildflowers. Sturdy juniper and pinyon dot the higher slopes. And in the distance, beyond the strange bee-line wrinkles of the San Andreas Fault, the Mojave Desert sprawls far and wide.

The Burkhart Trail, built years ago by a rancher of that name, is the only maintained footpath onto Pleasant View Ridge. The trail ascends the steep west slopes of Cruthers Creek from the desert to Burkhart Saddle, a distinct gap on the crest between Will Thrall Peak and Pallett Mountain. Except in a few places, it is gently graded as it climbs steadily from joshua tree and sage through a pinyon forest, and finally into Jeffrey pine country along the ridgetop.

The Burkhart Trail is a fitting introduction to the desert side of the San Gabriels, a side not well known to most Southern California hikers.

Description

Drive to Pearblossom on State Highway 138, then south and southeast on County Road N6 to Devils Punchbowl County Park, 8 miles.

The new trailhead is at the County Park, thereby avoiding the private property trespass of the old Lewis Ranch trailhead. Walk south through the picnic area and pick up the trail as it passes behind the silver water tank and climbs the slope immediately west of Punchbowl Canyon. In ½ mile you reach a dirt road. Ascend the road, veering right at a Y junction, to the new lateral trail above the Devils Punchbowl. Turn right (a sign says BURKHART TRAIL, 1½ MILES) and follow the new trail as it contours the mountain slope through Jeffrey pine and manzanita. You drop into Cruthers Creek and intersect the old trail coming up from Lewis Ranch, then climb the west slope and traverse upward high above the creek, through pinyon. You pass a small spring (water only in rainy season) and finally reach Burkhart Saddle, from where you look down into Little Rock Creek.

You now have several options. You can return to where you started. You can climb a faint trail leading right (west) up Pleasant View Ridge, around Will Thrall Peak, ending on a small flat on the crest (1½ miles from the saddle). Or you can descend south from Burkhart Saddle into Little Rock Creek and on up to Buckhorn on the Angeles Crest Highway (see Trip 63). Another option is to continue east, on your return, on the new High Desert Trail across the top of Devils Punchbowl to South Fork Campground (see Trip 69). All these options require a car shuttle. ▲

68 Devils Punchbowl County Park— Loop Trip

HIKE LENGTH:	1 mile; 300' elevation loss and gain
CLASSIFICATION:	Easy
SEASON:	October-June
TOPO MAP:	Valyermo

Features

The great San Andreas Rift Zone cuts a bee-line swath along the desert side of the San Gabriels. Many interesting geological features lie along this monumental earthquake fault system, but none so strange as the fantastic jumble of whitish rocks known as the Devils Punchbowl. Within this mile-wide depression rise row upon row of weathered sandstone blocks, many of them tilted so as to resemble plates standing on edge, others folded and broken like huge slices of fancy pudding.

In 1963 this unique geological formation became a Los Angeles County Park. A paved road was built to its western rim, and a wide, well-graded loop trail hacked out down into the bowl.

Although only a short down-and-up walk, this hike into the Devils Punchbowl is one of the most interesting trips in the range. The trail passes beside weird sandstone outcroppings, and at the bottom of the bowl, a playful stream cascades over, around and through the slanted formations. Hardy pinyons and manzanita thickets cling to precipitous footholds between the rocks. It's almost as if you were in a different world.

Description

Drive to Pearblossom on State Highway 138, then south and southeast on County Road N6 to Devils Punchbowl County Park, 8 miles.

From the parking area, walk east past the park headquarters (rest rooms, picnic tables, interpretive displays) to the well-marked beginning of the trail. Follow the trail as it winds 300' down into the punchbowl, turns right just above the bottom, and then ascends back up to the parking area. The trail is gently graded for the most part (one short steep pitch on the way out), and well worth the stride down and the huff-and-puff back out just to see first-hand what nature, in a fit of originality, has wrought. ▲

69

South Fork Campground to Devils Punchbowl

HIKE LENGTH:	6 miles round trip; 1000' elevation gain
CLASSIFICATION:	Moderate
SEASON:	October-June
TOPO MAP:	Valyermo

Features

This trail trip climbs over a ridge and enters the "back door" of the Devils Punchbowl. It visits the wilder eastern part of the jumbled depression, a section not reached by the newer loop trail from County Park headquarters (Trip 68). It takes you to the strangest, most unique formation in the punchbowl—the huge white rock mass, sheer on three sides, known as the Devil's Chair. Those with vivid imaginations can make out the Devil himself sitting on his throne, lording it over his topsy-turvy domain.

You may wish to continue westward across the top of the Punchbowl on the newly rebuilt High Desert Trail, then north on the Burkhart Trail connection to Park headquarters. With a 6-mile car shuttle, you can hike clear across the park and see it all.

Description

From State Highway 138, turn south at Pearblossom onto Longview Road, then left (southeast) on Valyermo Road past Valyermo, and right (south) on Big Rock Creek Road. Roughly 2½ miles from this junction, turn south on a marked dirt road to South Fork Campground, 1 mile. Leave your car in the hikers' parking area, to your left about 100 yards before the campground.

Follow the well-marked trail north about 50 yards to a junction, where you turn right (west), cross the boulderstrewn creekbed and climb through pinyon, scrub oak, manzanita and mountain mahogany to a saddle on the ridge. You contour, then drop into Holcomb Canyon. Here you find a rare meeting of three plant communities: pine, pinyon-juniper and streamside woodland. By late spring the yuccas are in full bloom. The trail fords tiny Holcomb Creek, then zigzigs over another ridge, skirting the upper section of the devil's domain. You pass near the huge rock promontory known as the Devil's Chair, where a breathtaking view of the punchbowl is obtained. If you venture onto the Devil's Chair, stay within the protective fence. You can explore other

The trail to Devils Punchbowl   W.R.C. Shendenhelm

geological features above the punchbowl, but don't venture too close to cliffs or steep slopes. If you're not sure-footed, stay on the trail.

Return the way you came. A very attractive option is to continue west on the High Desert Trail, traversing the forest-clad slopes above the Punchbowl, to the Burkhart Trail connection, and turn north on the latter down to Park Headquarters, 5.8 miles. You need a car shuttle for this (see Trip 67). ▲

70 South Fork Trail—South Fork Campground to Islip Saddle

HIKE LENGTH:	10 miles round trip; 2100' elevation gain
CLASSIFICATION:	Moderate
SEASON:	All year (upper part may be snowbound after winter storms)
TOPO MAPS:	Valyermo, Crystal Lake

Features

The north front of the San Gabriel Mountains rises abruptly out of the desert, especially the parts north of the middle and eastern high country. Some of the canyons that incise this rampart are quite imposing, being deep, V-shaped gorges. Probably the most impressive of these north-facing canyons is the South Fork of Big Rock Creek, which carves a steep path as it drops from high on the Angeles Crest down into the San Andreas Rift region at the foot of the mountains.

An old trail—once a major route into the high country, before the Angeles Crest Highway forever changed the face of the mountains— climbs up-canyon all the way from South Fork Campground to Islip Saddle, passing from pinyon to pine, from sage to snow brush, from cactus to buckthorn. The trail is seldom trod nowadays, for it culminates at that busy trans-mountain thoroughfare, the Angeles Crest Highway. But its lower and middle parts hold appeal—the foliage a curious blend of desert and alpine, the landscape often more vertical than horizontal.

Description

Drive to South Fork Public Campground (for directions, see Trip 69). Leave your car at the indicated parking area just below the campground.

Walk south on the well-marked trail, going left at a junction with the trail to Devils Punchbowl, passing South Fork Campground on your left, and entering the deep canyon of Big Rock Creek's South Fork. Follow the trail up-canyon, through spruce, oak, maple and alder, alongside the boulder-strewn streambed. After ¼ mile the trail crosses to the west bank and begins climbing the canyon slopes, through scattered pinyon pines. Pinyon soon gives way to Jeffrey as you climb higher, with the bubbling creek far down to your left. After about 4 miles you pass trickling Reed Spring, then climb 1 more short mile to the parking area alongside the Angeles Crest Highway at Islip Saddle. ▲

71 West Fork of the San Gabriel River, Highway 39 to Glenn Trail Camp, Cogswell Dam and Reservoir

HIKE LENGTH:	16 miles round trip; 800' elevation gain
CLASSIFICATION:	Strenuous (1 day); Moderate (2 days)
SEASON:	All year
TOPO MAPS:	Glendora, Azusa

Features

The mountain watershed of the San Gabriel River can be compared to a colossal live oak, standing squat on a stout trunk, with an erect center limb and long horizontal branches extending outward in both directions. The great branch extending almost straight westward is known to thousands of hikers, campers and anglers simply as the West Fork.

The West Fork cuts a deep V-shaped trench, separating the front range from the high country to the north. Fed by the waters of numerous tributaries, an all-year stream graces the canyon bowels, shaded much of the way by oak, alder, maple and spruce. Some of the densest chaparral in the range blankets the north slopes of the West Fork, while the steeper south flanks are covered with big-cone spruce.

Since civilized humans first entered the San Gabriels, the West Fork has been an angler's delight—more so in the past than today. One historian has written: "The waters of the West Fork were so loaded with fish that in 1892 Frank Bolt, president of the San Gabriel Valley Bank, caught one hundred trout in one pool and then became so carried away with his success that he fell in."

This trip leaves Highway 39 where it bridges the West Fork and follows the streamside fire road 8 miles up-canyon to Glenn Trail Camp and Cogswell Dam. If you're going all the way, it's best to make the trip a backpack and stay the night at the shady trail camp. Fishing is allowed on the West Fork up to the second bridge; beyond, it's catch-and-release fishing only. No fishing is permitted in Cogswell Reservoir.

Description

Drive up Highway 39 to the parking area adjacent to the highway bridge crossing the West Fork, 1½ miles from Azusa, 1 mile past Rincon Ranger Station. There is a $3 parking fee in San Gabriel Canyon on weekends, payable at the Forest Service canyon entrance station.

On the south side of the bridge, pass a locked gate and walk west up the fire road that follows the streamside. In a mile you pass the junction of the Bear Creek Trail, leading up into the San Gabriel Wilderness (see Trip 74). Just beyond you cross a bridge to the north bank. Follow it awhile, then recross the stream and follow the shadier south bank the rest of the way. You pass the rugged portals of Big Mermaids and Little Mermaids canyons, trailless and inaccessible parts of the San Gabriel Wilderness. (The West Fork here serves as the south boundary of the Wilderness.) After 4 miles the canyon narrows and the sidewalls steepen, with sheer rock cliffs here and there. In 7 miles you reach Glenn Trail Camp, nestled in a woodsy recess where Glenn Canyon intersects the main stream—stoves and tables. One mile farther is Cogswell Dam and Reservoir, built in the '30s for flood control.

A short cross-country side trip can be made to the Falls of Glenn Canyon, ¼ mile up from Glenn Trail Camp. They are three cascades, one right above the other, in the densely wooded canyon. To see all three at once, climb about 30 feet up the west slope opposite the lower fall. In times of high water, these are the most spectacular falls in the range.

Return the way you came. ▲

72 Highway 39 to Bichota Canyon

HIKE LENGTH: 6 miles round trip; 1200' elevation gain
CLASSIFICATION: Easy to Moderate
SEASON: November-May
TOPO MAP: Crystal Lake

Features

Bichota Canyon is once again worth visiting. Nature's redemptive powers have restored much of the sylvan beauty of the canyon, so badly marred in the terrible 1969 fire. Chaparral again clothes the hillsides, and the sparkling all-year creek is shaded, much of the way, by majestic live oak, alder, sycamore and a few big-cone spruce.

Although the Forest Service no longer maintains the canyon trail, the walk up Bichota Canyon is a delight, particularly on a cool fall or spring day. You follow the creek all the way to the canyon head, crossing via easy boulder-hops many times, alternating between sunshine and shade. Few hikers use this trail, so you are likely to have the upper canyon all to yourself.

Description

Drive up Highway 39 to Bichota Mesa, 14 miles from Azusa, 2½ miles above the junction of the West and North forks of the San Gabriel River. Park on the right (east) side of the highway about 100 yards beyond the locked gate to the Bichota Canyon Road.

Walk past the locked gate and down the canyon access road, crossing the North Fork of the San Gabriel on a concrete bridge and, 50 yards beyond, Bichota Creek by boulder hopping. About 50 yards from road's end, amid a cluster of private cabins, go left and cross to the north side of Bichota Creek via a wooden bridge. Here you pick up the trail leading up-canyon just above the creek, passing three more cabins. In about 200 yards your path fords the creek and then follows a wooded bench above the south bank for ¼ mile before dropping to the creek once again. The trail now becomes difficult to follow as it continues up-canyon, fording the creek many times, 3 miles to the canyon head. However, the going is relatively easy if you don't mind boulder hopping and the many stream crossings.

Note: Forest Adventure Pass required.

There is a shooting area on the ridge north of Bichota Canyon, so the peace and quiet of the area are often disturbed, particularly on weekends and holidays. Best do this trip on a weekday, when shooters are usually not there. ▲

73 Highway 39 to Smith Mountain

HIKE LENGTH:	7 miles round trip; 1900' elevation gain
CLASSIFICATION:	Moderate
SEASON:	October-June
TOPO MAP:	Crystal Lake

Features

5111' Smith Mountain stands tall on the divide separating the North Fork of the San Gabriel River from Bear Creek, smack on the eastern boundary of the rugged San Gabriel Wilderness. From its summit you get a bird's-eye view over the eastern half of the primitive area, with the deep chasm of Bear Creek right below you. Looming close on the northwest skyline are the rocky battlements of Twin Peaks Ridge, one of the last citadels of bighorn sheep in this range. The sheep were once prevalent in the range; now only a few survivors make a last stand in the most isolated parts of the mountains.

The climb is mostly by trail, but the last 800' rise is a steep ridge scramble, partly through brush, to the summit. Wear lug-soled boots.

Description

Drive up Highway 39 to the beginning of the Bear Creek Trail, marked by a metal sign, 17 miles from Azusa, ¼ mile before Coldbrook Camp. Leave your car in the parking area at the trailhead, on the left (west) side of the road.

Walk 3 miles up the well-graded Bear Creek Trail to Smith Saddle at the top of the ridge. From the saddle, leave the trail and scramble left (south) directly up the ridge, following traces of a path beaten by climbers. In some spots you must thrash through light brush. You reach the summit in ½ mile.

After taking in the superb view, return the same way. Watch your footing during the ridge descent. ▲

74 San Gabriel Wilderness— Highway 39 to Smith Saddle, Bear Creek, West Fork of San Gabriel River

HIKE LENGTH:	11 miles one way; 1100' elevation gain, 2800' loss
CLASSIFICATION:	Moderate to Strenuous
SEASON:	October-June
TOPO MAPS:	Crystal Lake, Waterman Mountain, Azusa, Glendora

Features

There are no trails through the San Gabriel Wilderness. There are only trails that touch its outer perimeter and gingerly probe a short distance into its primitive sanctuary. The heart of this wilderness remains as wild as ever. The footpath that penetrates the farthest into the San Gabriel Wilderness is the Bear Creek Trail, which forges an 11-mile semicircle through the southeastern corner of the region.

The highlight of this trail trip is the 4-mile stretch along lower Bear Creek. This is the tamer part of the canyon. A delightful stream dances and cascades under tall stands of big-cone spruce, alder and oak, interspaced with open chaparral glades. There are grassy flats where the canyon widens, and rock-ribbed corridors where it narrows. Most of all there is a feel of wildness. Nature reigns here; humans are the intruders.

The upper two thirds of Bear Creek, beyond where the trail comes down from Smith Saddle, is trailless and virtually inaccessible unless you're an experienced mountaineer. You can scramble about a ¼ mile up-canyon without too much difficulty, but then you reach the gorge. Here granite sidewalls close in and steepen, and waterfalls assume more impressive proportions. This is where nature says stop, you've come far enough, leave the rest to me.

Once this was bear country, but you almost never see them now. Around the turn of the century, hunters came in and shot them by the dozen. Pasadena historian Hiram Reid told of one such incident, which resulted in the name for the canyon: "In 1891 or 92 two or three hunters camped in the upper part of this canyon. One night a bear was caught

Falls on Bear Creek   Louise Werner

by the hind foot in a heavy steel trap which they had set. He gnawed off his own leg and hobbled away on the bleeding stump, leaving his foot in the trap. The hunters soon discovered this in the morning, and following the bear's trail, shot him. They nailed the entrapped foot up on a tree at their camp, and I saw it there about two years later. From this incident that portion of the West San Gabriel has ever since been called 'Bear Canyon'.

Today there are three wilderness campsites along the lower creek, spaced about a mile apart on shady streamside benches. These were once trail camps with stoves and fire rings, but they were so badly vandalized that the Forest Service removed all the facilities. However, they still make good overnight campsites. The trip can be done in a leisurely fashion, staying the night at one of the wilderness camps, or it can be done strenuously in one long day.

A 6-mile car shuttle is necessary to do the whole trip, or you can go part way in and return by the same route. Wear lug-soled boots for the many stream crossings and the stretches of boulder-hopping where the trail fades out.

Description

Drive up Highway 39 to the junction of the North and West forks of the San Gabriel River, 11½ miles from Azusa. Leave one car here in the wide parking area, and drive the other 6 miles farther up the North Fork to the beginning of the Bear Creek Trail (so indicated by a metal sign). If you pass Coldbrook Campground, you've driven ¼ mile too far. Park on the west side of the road at the trailhead.

Walk up the Bear Creek Trail to Smith Saddle at the top of the ridge, then down the other side to the creek at Upper Bear wilderness campsite, 6 miles in. This is a hot 6 miles, as it is almost entirely through chaparral, with little shade, but when you reach Bear Creek you're in the forest. The trail camp here stretches along the east bank, with little shaded flats for sleeping. The trail continues down-canyon, disappearing in boulder areas, only to reappear a short distance beyond on the opposite bank. In slightly over a mile you reach West Fork Bear wilderness campsite, shaded by alders, back a ways from the creek. Here the wild, trailless defile of Bear Creek's West Fork, plunging down from Twin Peaks, adds its waters to the mainstream. Continuing down the canyon, you emerge from forest cover and scramble across boulders where the creek turns into a rocky wash. Then you pass under oaks and alders to Bear Creek wilderness campsite. Below this, the canyon widens and the trail becomes more distinct, crossing grassy flats and passing under scattered oaks and alders. Ten miles from the start, 4 miles from where you first reached Bear Creek, you arrive at the broad

West Fork of the San Gabriel River. Cross the river, either by boulder-hopping or detouring a hundred yards west to a concrete bridge, and follow the fire road east 1 mile to Highway 39. ▲

75 Soldier Creek Trail— Highway 39 to Lewis Falls

HIKE LENGTH:	1 mile round trip; 250' elevation gain
CLASSIFICATION:	Easy
SEASON:	All year
TOPO MAP:	Crystal Lake

Features

Green, woodsy Soldier Creek is a place of sylvan enchantment. Tucked away under high ridges in the upper reaches of the San Gabriel's North Fork, the creek seldom suffers the full glare of sunlight. Its singing waters glide and dance and tumble beneath overarching oaks, sycamores and alders. In summer, when the surrounding country is hot and dry, the little canyon of Soldier Creek is a damp and verdant oasis.

The trail is short—only ½ mile from the highway crossing to Lewis Falls (named for the late district ranger Anselmo Lewis)—but it makes up in delightful quality what it lacks in quantity. It is a place to saunter and rest and contemplate, and to return from refreshed and revitalized.

Description

Drive up Highway 39 to the unmarked Soldier Creek crossing, 2-½ miles above Coldbrook Camp, 19½ miles from Azusa. If you pass Falling Springs Resort, you've gone a hundred yards too far. Leave the car in the dirt parking area to the right of the road.

Follow the unmarked trail up the right (east) side of the creek, passing a number of privately leased summer cabins. The trail fades out beyond the last cabin, slightly less than ½ mile from the highway. Scramble over boulders, crossing and recrossing the creek for about 200 yards to the small clearing at the bottom of 50' high Lewis Falls.

Return the same way. ▲

76 Crystal Lake to Little Jimmy Spring, Mt. Islip

HIKE LENGTH: 7 miles round trip; 2200' elevation gain
CLASSIFICATION: Moderate
SEASON: June-October
TOPO MAP: Crystal Lake

Features

Mount Islip (pronounced "eye-slip") rises in relative isolation at the west end of the middle high country. From its 8250' summit, ridges descend south to separate Crystal Lake basin from Bear Canyon, west down to Islip Saddle, and east to Windy Gap and the high country beyond. Because its cone-shaped summit stands apart from the other peaks of the mountain backbone, the hiker is rewarded with an unusually fine panorama over the heart of the San Gabriels.

The mountain was named for George Islip, an early mountain pioneer who homesteaded in San Gabriel Canyon during the 1880s. In 1909 students from Occidental College, who had a summer cabin at Pine Flats (the old name for Crystal Lake basin), built a huge rock and wood cairn with the name "Occidental" on top. For many years this "Occidental Monument" was a well-known landmark to hikers. In 1927 the Forest Service removed the old monument to make way for a fire lookout tower, which in turn was moved to South Mt. Hawkins a decade later. Today, a dilapidated old stone cabin, just below the summit, remains as a lone reminder of those days when searching eyes guarded the high country.

Deep in the forest, snug under the east ridge of Mt. Islip, is Little Jimmy Spring. Old-timers knew this miniature, trickling water course as Gooseberry Spring, for the many wild gooseberry bushes that once surrounded it. By this name it was known when Jim Swinnerton, famed cartoonist, camped nearby in the summer of 1909. Swinnerton's "Little Jimmy" comic strip was enjoyed by Sunday newspaper readers across the nation. Passers-by that summer were often rewarded with "Little Jimmy" sketches by the camping cartoonist. Since then, the little spring and nearby campground have been known as "Little Jimmy."

This is a circle trip, ascending via the old Windy Gap trail, and descending by the new Islip Ridge Trail and Big Cienaga Cutoff, completed by the volunteer San Gabriel Mountain Trail Builders in 1990.

Description

Drive to the upper (northern) edge of the Crystal Lake Recreation Area, 25 miles from Azusa on Highway 39. Park in the large dirt clearing to your right just before the locked gate.

The trailhead is marked by a metal sign across the road from the parking area. Follow the trail as it makes a gradual ascent through oak, pine and cedar, crosses two switchbacks of the South Mt. Hawkins fire road, and reaches a junction with the new Big Cienaga Cutoff. Go right and follow the old trail as it zigzags up the steep slope to Windy Gap, 2 miles. Go left (northwest) at the Windy Gap trail junction. You immediately reach another junction with the shortcut trail going up to Mt. Islip. If your destination is the mountaintop, go left. For Little Jimmy Trail Camp continue straight ahead. Your trail contours along the slope, passes just above Little Jimmy Spring (unsafe to drink), and rounds a bend to Little Jimmy Trail Camp, ½ mile from Windy Gap. Here are stoves, tables, restrooms, and plenty of little shaded flats for overnight campers.

Return to the afore-mentioned trail junction. Go right and follow the Islip Ridge Trail east down the ridgetop, then southwest down the Big Cienaga Cutoff to its junction with the Windy Gap Trail, 3 miles. Descend the latter to the roadhead. ▲

77 Islip Saddle to Little Jimmy Campground and Mt. Islip

HIKE LENGTH: 7 miles round trip; 1500' elevation gain
CLASSIFICATION: Easy to Moderate
SEASON: June-October
TOPO MAP: Crystal Lake

Features

This is a scenic way to reach Little Jimmy Campground and to climb Mt. Islip, starting from Islip Saddle on the Angeles Crest Highway and utilizing a section of the Pacific Crest Trail. The route has far-ranging views out over the desert and is shaded by magnificent Jeffrey and sugar pines much of the way.

Description

Drive to Islip Saddle on the Angeles Crest Highway, 41 miles from La Canada (Mileage marker 64). Park in the large clearing to the left (north) of the highway.

Cross the highway and pick up the Pacific Crest Trail leading east. Follow the well-graded trail as it climbs through chaparral, then into pines, to Little Jimmy Campground, 2½ miles. The campground is an ideal stop for overnight backpackers, located in a secluded little forest shallow, with stoves and rest rooms. About ¼ mile southeast by trail is Little Jimmy Spring, where water is always available.

A sign near the west end of the campground points the way to Mt. Islip. The trail switchbacks ½ mile up to the east ridge, then follows the ridge another ½ mile, passing a junction with the new Islip Ridge Trail, to the summit. Return by the same route.

An alternate route is to start from Islip Saddle, 1½ miles farther west on the Angeles Crest Highway, and follow the historic old crest trail as it winds its way through dense, thorny snowbrush to meet the fire road in 1½ miles, then walk a mile farther on the road to Little Jimmy Campground. The route up Mt. Islip is the same as above. ▲

78 Middle High Country—Crystal Lake to Windy Gap, Mt. Hawkins, Throop Peak, Mt. Baden-Powell

HIKE LENGTH:	17 miles round trip; 3300' elevation gain
CLASSIFICATION:	Strenuous
SEASON:	June-October
TOPO MAP:	Crystal Lake

Features

The middle high country—so named because of its central location along the main backbone of the San Gabriels—rises as a long, sinuous rooftop over the many-pronged watershed of the San Gabriel River. Along this divide stands a progression of rounded summits, rising from just over 8000' in the west to over 9000' at its eastern terminus. From west to east, the major high points are Mt. Islip, Mt. Hawkins, Throop Peak, Mt. Burnham, and finally 9399' Mt. Baden-Powell.

This trail trip climbs around or over all of these summits save Islip (and this peak you can surmount also with a short detour) as it traverses almost the length of the backbone. The trail is long, with few level stretches, but it is well-maintained and easy to follow. This is delightful summer or fall hiking country. The high mountain breeze is cool and refreshing. The forest monarchs here are greener and healthier than their brethren on the smog-assaulted south slopes of the range.

The chaparral is knee-high and in clumps, not smothering the terrain as it does on lower slopes. Over near Baden-Powell, on wind-buffeted ridges, are a handful of gnarled, weather-battered limber pines, hardy relies of a bygone age, found only on a handful of our highest summits.

Description

Drive to the upper (northern) edge of the Crystal Lake Recreation Area, 25 miles from Azusa on Highway 39.

The beginning of the trail is marked by a metal sign indicating WINDY GAP TRAIL. Follow the trail as it ascends gradually through oak, pine and cedar, crosses two switch-backs of the South Hawkins Lookout fire road, and zigzags steeply up the mountain slope to Windy Gap. Here is a major trail junction—left to Little Jimmy and Mt. Islip (see Trip 76), right to Baden-Powell. Turn right (east) and follow the trail as it climbs steadily along the north slope of the main divide. As

Limber pines on Mt. Baden-Powell

you top 8400', the forest changes from predominately Jeffrey pine to lodgepole. Two miles from Windy Gap, just below Mt. Hawkins, a side trail drops 240' in ½ mile to secluded Lily Spring, the only water enroute. The main trail contours along the northwest slope of Hawkins (250' up to the summit, a short but steep scramble), drops to a saddle, and climbs the southwest ridge of Throop before traversing around the southeast side of the peak (again, just below the top, which lies a short distance away up a climbers' path), and turns eastward toward Mt. Baden-Powell, now looming massively on the skyline.

From here you go down across another saddle, around the north side of a forested slight bump known as Mt. Burnham, to still another saddle and around one more unnamed welt, and finally begin the climb of Baden-Powell. As you rise above 9000', the forest thins and you pass several ancient limber pines. Just north of the top you intersect the Baden-Powell summit trail; from here walk up two short switchbacks and you're there. On the nearly bald crown is a Boy Scout monument (see Trip 81), a metal register, and a weathered flagpole. The view is well worth the long trip: Old Baldy dominates the eastern skyline beyond the yawning chasm of the East Fork; to the south, progressively lower ridge lines disappear into haze; westward is an end-on perspective of the middle high country you've just traversed; and northward sprawls the drab emptiness of the Mojave Desert.

Return the same way or, if you can talk someone into driving around to the Angeles Crest Highway, you can take the short trail down to Vincent Gap (see Trip 81). This would shorten the 17-mile round trip to 12½ miles.

Another alternate is to start and finish on the Angeles Crest Highway. Drive to Islip Saddle and follow the Pacific Crest Trail to Little Jimmy Campground (see Trip 77). Then continue on the PCT past Windy Gap on the trail described above. Then return the same way. This alternate is the same total hiking distance, but it requires 800 feet less elevation gain. ▲

79 Crystal Lake to Mt. Hawkins and South Mt. Hawkins Lookout

HIKE LENGTH: 12 miles round trip; 2800' elevation gain

CLASSIFICATION: Moderate

SEASON: June-October

TOPO MAP: Crystal Lake

Features

Never a gal like Nellie Hawkins, beautiful waitress at "Doc" Beatty's popular Squirrel Inn, high up the North Fork of San Gabriel Canyon where Coldbrook Campground lies today. From 1901 to about 1907, Miss Hawkins charmed and attracted miners, hunters, campers—just about every mountain man for miles around. Nellie is long gone now, and the doors of Squirrel Inn have been closed for half a century, but the popular waitress will never be forgotten. Her name is eternally transfixed on two summits above Crystal Lake Basin, and two other high points along the same ridge honor her informally. The two officially named peaks are "Mt. Hawkins" and "South Mt. Hawkins" the two bumps on the ridge between are known to hikers as "Middle Hawkins" and, facetiously, "Sadie Hawkins."

This circle trip climbs over or around all four of Nellie's namesakes in covering the high country northeast and east of Crystal Lake. The highlight of the trip is following the new trail, built by Charles Jones and his San Gabriel Trailbuilders, along the ridge between Mt. Hawkins and South Hawkins Lookout road, with spectacular views both ways—into the Crystal Lake Basin to the west, and across the wild, trailless Iron Fork country to the east.

Except for the short scramble up Mt. Hawkins, the trip is all on trail or fire road.

Description

Drive to the upper (northern) edge of the Crystal Lake Recreation Area, 25 miles from Azusa on Highway 39.

Take the Windy Gap Trail (see Trip 76) to the gap (2½ miles). At the gap turn right (east) and follow the Pacific Crest Trail as it climbs steadily toward Mt. Hawkins. Continue on the trail as it traverses along the northwest slope of Mt. Hawkins. The easiest route to the summit lies along the northeast spur, so you are better off to stay on the trail just past the peak, and then double back and up.

Return to the Pacific Crest Trail and backtrack west about ¼ mile to the junction with the recently built Hawkins Trail. Turn left (south) and follow the trail down the ridge, around the intervening bumps known to hikers as "Middle Hawkins" and "Sadie Hawkins," until you meet the fire road. Follow the latter ⅓ mile up to the South Hawkins Lookout tower.

Descend the road down the Jeffrey-forested west slope to Crystal Lake Campground—5 miles. ▲

80 Dawson Saddle to Throop Peak

HIKE LENGTH:	4½ miles round trip; 1200' elevation gain
CLASSIFICATION:	Moderate
SEASON:	June-October
TOPO MAP:	Crystal Lake

Features

The Angeles Crest Highway winds through the heart of the San Gabriels like an elongated snake, reaching its highest point at 7901' Dawson Saddle. From this saddle, a prominent ridge ascends southward, reaching the crest at Throop Peak (9138') (pronounced "Troop" named for Amos G. Throop [1811-1894], founder of Cal Tech).

A recently rebuilt trail climbs this ridge, then contours around the north slope of Throop Peak to a junction with the Pacific Crest Trail just east of the summit ridge, passing through an open forest of Jeffrey pine, white fir and—higher up—lodgepole pine. Most of the route offers wide-ranging views of the north-side high country and the desert far below.

This trip, climbing the rebuilt trail to the Pacific Crest Trail, then ascending the south slope of Throop Peak to the summit, is one of the best in the San Gabriel high country. Do it on a warm summer or an early fall day, when panoramas are far-reaching and the crisp high-mountain air is refreshing and invigorating.

Description

Drive to Dawson Saddle on the Angeles Crest Highway, 5½ miles east of Islip Saddle (49 miles from La Canada; Mileage marker 69.5). Park in the large clearing north of the road.

The old trail switchbacks up the ridge directly across the highway from the Dawson Saddle parking area. The new route begins about 150 yards down the highway to the east. Take either trail; they join atop the ridge in ¼ mile. You walk through an open pine forest, first atop the ridge, then along the east slope, gently climbing southward. In 1½ miles, the old and new trails part company: The old route goes right and climbs steeply up the ridge to Throop's summit; you go left on the new trail as it contours, then climbs around the north slope of Throop Peak to an unmarked junction with the Pacific Crest Trail, 2 miles from the start. Turn right and follow the PCT ¼ mile to a climbers path on the south side of the peak. Follow this path to the summit—steep but easy going.

You have a choice of routes on the return. You can, of course, descend the same way you came up. Or you can take the old but well-trod route that drops, steeply at first, down the northwest ridge, joining the new trail in ½ mile. Other options, requiring car shuttles, are to follow the PCT east to Mt. Baden-Powell and down to Vincent Gap (Trip 81), or go west on the PCT down to Windy Gap, Little Jimmy Campground, and Islip Saddle (Trip 77). ▲

81 Vincent Gap to Mt. Baden-Powell

HIKE LENGTH:	8 miles round trip; 2800' elevation gain
CLASSIFICATION:	Moderate
SEASON:	June-October
TOPO MAP:	Crystal Lake

Features

Next to Old Baldy, Baden-Powell (9399') is probably the most popular mountain climb in the San Gabriels. A superb trail climbs directly up the northeast ridge to the summit in 41 switchbacks (the most of any trail in the range), with panoramic views north over the Mojave Desert and southeast into the deep chasm of the East Fork, San Gabriel River. The trip is a living demonstration of how the forest changes with altitude: from oak and Jeffrey pine, through white fir, into lodgepole, and finally a scattering of ancient, gnarled limber pines clinging to bare slopes above 9000 feet.

For many years the peak was known as North Baldy. In 1931 the Forest Service and U.S. Board on Geographic Names sanctioned a request by C. J. Carlson, Western Regional Boy Scout Director, to rename the peak after Lord Robert Stevenson Smyth Baden-Powell (1847-1941), a British Army officer who founded the Boy Scout movement in 1907. The official dedication of the new name took place on May 30, 1931, when a large party of Los Angeles area Boy Scouts erected a plaque and flagpole on the summit. Three years later, CCC workers constructed the present 4-mile zigzagging trail from Vincent Gap to the top.

For the next 2½ decades the peak was all but forgotten by the Scouts; the plaque disappeared and the flagstaff became bent and rusted. This sad situation was brought to the attention of Michael H. "Wally" Waldron, member of the executive board of the L.A. Area Council of the Boy Scouts. Under Waldron's inspiration, over 2000 Scouts took part in a 9-week project to erect a permanent bronze-and-cement monument on the summit. The official re-dedication took place on September 28, 1957. Since then, Scouts have made an annual "Silver Moccasin" pilgrimage across the San Gabriels to the peak. On the summit ridge is a grove of 2000-year-old, weather-bent limber pines, discovered by Angeles National Forest Supervisor Sim Jarvi in 1962. One of the largest specimens is named the "Waldron Tree," in honor of the volunteer Scout leader who organized the Boy Scout homage to the mountaintop.

Description

Leave your car at the Vincent Gap parking area on the Angeles Crest Highway, 53 miles from La Canada, or 5½ from Big Pines.

A large wooden sign indicates BADEN-POWELL TRAIL—4 MILES. The trail starts up wooden steps, then switchbacks upward through a lush forest of oak and Jeffrey pine, with a scattering of sugar pine and incense cedar also dotting the slopes. It continues climbing steadily up the long northeast ridge of the mountain. At 1½ miles an unmarked side trail leads left (southeast) 200 yards to Lamel Spring, the only water enroute. At about 2 miles, white fir begins to pre-dominate, and shortly beyond that, the first lodgepoles appear. As the trail tops 8000' the view opens out to the north, where the tawny expanse of the Mojave Desert fades into distant desert ranges. Now the forest thins and becomes almost exclusively lodgepole pine, tall and erect. The trail steepens, and the switchbacks shorten.

At 3½ miles (9000') the first aged, gnarled limber pines are encountered. A small sign points right (southwest) to a limber pine forest, 300 yards on a side trail. Four switchbacks beyond, the trail abruptly emerges atop the ridge, with spectacular views eastward into the Prairie Fork of the San Gabriel, and the gray bulk of Old Baldy on the skyline. Just before the final climb to the summit, the crest trail branches off to the right; its sign indicates 6 miles to Little Jimmy Spring, 9 miles to Crystal Lake. Two more switchbacks, past scattered limber pine and lodgepole, and the trail reaches the 9399' summit, with its Boy

Scout monument, metal register box (usually full) and flagpole. The panorama is well worth the climb (providing the lower atmosphere is not clogged with brown murkiness): a vast expanse of mountain, desert and lowland scenery.

Return the same way. ▲

82 Vincent Gap to Big Horn Mine

HIKE LENGTH:	4 miles round trip; 500′ elevation gain
CLASSIFICATION:	Easy
SEASON:	June-October
TOPO MAPS:	Crystal Lake, Mount San Antonio

Features

Gold mining—both placer and lode—has played a long and prominent part in the saga of human beings in the San Gabriels. One of the most famous of the lode mines was the Big Horn, perched at 6900′ on the rocky east slopes of Mt. Baden-Powell. Its weather-battered, crumbling remains are among the most photogenic reminders of the once-feverish mining era in the mountains.

From Vincent Gap, a wide trail (the remains of an old wagon road) contours around the massive east flank of Baden-Powell to the mine ruins. The route, shaded by stands of Jeffrey pine and white fir, offers an almost continuous panorama down into the East Fork of the San Gabriel, with Baldy and its sister peaks rising as a massive backdrop. This is an ideal trip for both the history buff and the shutter enthusiast.

It was mountain man Charles Tom Vincent, a fugitive whose real name was Charles Vincent Daugherty, who discovered the Big Horn in 1894—the climax of a years-long search for the lode that fed the rich placers of the East Fork. Vincent, prospector and hunter who lived from about 1870 until 1926 in a crude log cabin high in Vincent Gulch, sold the mine to a group of investors, who spent a fortune to develop it. Thousands of feet of tunnels were bored, and heavy equipment was laboriously hauled in.

For slightly more than a decade the Big Horn prospered. The California Division of Mines reported a yield of nearly $40,000 in gold during 1904-1906. But, as with all San Gabriel mining ventures, the veins petered out and the effort was abandoned. In recent years, exploratory work has been done at the Big Horn, during which the gate was locked and NO TRESPASSING signs posted. As of this writing

(October 1997), the gate is open and the mine is not being worked. You may wish to check with the Forest Service before you attempt this historic trip, because the future of this hike is uncertain.

Description

Leave your car at the Vincent Gap parking area on the Angeles Crest Highway, 53 miles over the range from La Canada, or 5½ miles up from Big Pines on the desert side.

The trail, distinctive but unmarked, leaves the Vincent Gap parking area, drops about 60′ and begins to contour southeast around the mountain. Much of it is shaded by tall Jeffrey pines and white firs, an occasional sugar pine rising above the others. The old wagon road is an easy walk except for a washout near the halfway point that may trouble beginners and young hikers. Just past the washout, you pass a small mine tunnel, the beginning of the Big Horn complex. As you round the massive buttress of Mt. Baden-Powell, the deep gorge of the East Fork, San Gabriel River and its tributary canyons come into full view; beyond looms the grayish mass of Old Baldy. The trail rises about 300′ to top a ridge, and passes the foundations of mine buildings. As

Big Horn Mine — stamp mill

you round a bend, the old stamp mill comes suddenly into view, clinging to the precipitous, rocky hillside. This is Big Horn Mine, and here the broad trail ends. The main tunnel is just behind and above the mill building; it extends several hundred feet into the mountain, is usually wet, and is unsafe to explore beyond the entrance. An old footpath, narrow and partly overgrown, continues about ½ mile farther around the mountain, passing several small prospects. The big mill building is dilapidated and dangerous to enter, as a NO TRESPASSING sign indicates. But don't be disappointed; the views from trail's end of the huge mill, and out over the gorge of the East Fork to Old Baldy, are well worth the trip. ▲

83 Vincent Gap via Vincent Gulch to Prairie Fork, East Fork of San Gabriel River

HIKE LENGTH: 6 miles round trip; 2000' elevation loss and gain

CLASSIFICATION: Moderate

SEASON: May-October

TOPO MAPS: Crystal Lake, Mount San Antonio

Features

If you don't care for the narrow, winding dirt road from Blue Ridge down into Prairie Fork (see Trip 88),this is the best way to reach the upper East Fork country. You leave the Angeles Crest Highway at Vincent Gap and descend the broad sloping **V** of Vincent Gulch 3 miles to the great bend, where the East Fork's main channel elbows east and becomes Prairie Fork. Nearby is Mine Gulch Trail Camp for overnight stayers. This trip is a favorite of anglers; some fine trout swim in this cold mountain stream.

This upper East Fork country is rich in history as well as scenic attraction. Charles "Tom" Vincent—mountain man, prospector, and hunter of bighorn sheep, grizzly bear and deer—settled here sometime before 1880. His rustic cabin, high up in Vincent Gulch, was filled with the horns and skulls of game he had shot. Prairie Fork was so-named because early settlers herded cattle there to feed on the rich grasses. It is said that two perpetrators of the 1857 Mormon Massacre in Utah built the first cabin in Prairie Fork, settling there to hide from the law. Around the turn of the century, gold was recovered from the rock walls of Prairie Fork at the Native Son Mine. The mine's six tunnels have been idle since the early 1920s.

Description

Leave your car at the Vincent Gap parking area on the Angeles Crest Highway, 53 miles over the range from La Canada, or 5½ miles up from Big Pines on the desert side.

The trail is unmarked and easily confused with the Big Horn Mine footpath (see Trip 82). You start out the same, but after about 100 yards you turn left and follow the angler's path down Vincent Gulch. The trail stays on the right (west) slope for awhile, then crosses the small creek and parallels it close to the east bank for most of the remaining distance down. When you reach Prairie Fork, go right (west) a few hundred yards to Mine Gulch Trail Camp (stoves and tables).

You have three options from here. You can return back up Vincent Gulch to your car. You can turn east and follow the Prairie Fork Trail 3 miles to the roadhead at Cabin Flat (see Trip 85). This will require a car shuttle. Or you can descend the East Fork through The Narrows to East Fork Ranger Station, 11 miles (see Trips 84 and 85). This last alternative requires an across-the-range car shuttle. ▲

84 East Fork, San Gabriel River— Ranger Station to The Narrows

HIKE LENGTH: 9 miles round trip; 1000' elevation gain

CLASSIFICATION: Moderate

SEASON: November-June

TOPO MAPS: Glendora, Crystal Lake, Mount San Antonio

Features

The saga of the East Fork of the San Gabriel can just about be summed up in one word—gold. The precious metal was discovered in the canyon gravels in 1854, and almost overnight the East Fork became a scene of frenzied activity. The only real gold-rush town in the San Gabriels—Eldoradoville—sprang up where the East Fork elbows north. It boasted three hotels and a half dozen saloons. Not much more is known about Eldoradoville, for the rustic boom town was washed away lock, stock, and barrel in the great flood of 1862. Placer gold was exhausted soon thereafter, and prospectors began searching nearby draws and hillsides for promising quartz veins. Their efforts were rewarded, and for the next half century lode gold was recovered from tunnels and shafts along canyonsides and well up on higher slopes. Place names in the area today commemorate the miners of yester-year—Heaton Flat, Trogden's, Allison Gulch, Shoemaker Canyon, to name a few.

The East Fork is quiet now, save for the rush of the stream and the rustling of oak and spruce leaves. Prospectors no longer burrow for hidden treasures. But the scars of the gold-mining efforts can be seen almost the length of the chasm. You must look up along canyon slopes to see these aged marks; all evidences of streamside mining activities have long since been erased by the torrential floods that periodically scour the streambed.

This is an interesting trip for more than historical reasons. The scenery here is monumental, on a scale seen nowhere else in the San Gabriels. The gorge of the East Fork cuts deep into the eastern high country, separating such giants of the range as Mt. Baden-Powell and Old Baldy. The rise from the floor of The Narrows (2800') to the top of Iron Mountain (8007') is 5200' in 1¾ horizontal miles! This is nature in its grandest proportions (at least by Southern California standards). And there is good trout fishing in the broad stream.

A word of warning: do not attempt this trip after heavy rains. There are numerous stream crossings enroute, and storms turn this usually bubbling creek into a raging torrent, dangerous if not impossible to ford.

Description

From Azusa drive up the San Gabriel Canyon Road 10 miles, then turn east on the East Fork Road and continue 8 more miles to the East Fork Ranger Station. Park just below the station.

Walk north along the roadbed that follows the high bench east of the river for ½ mile before dropping to the canyon floor. Your trail now follows the river, fording its shallow but rushing waters fourteen times. You pass remnants of the old East Fork Road, a paved highway to The Narrows that was destroyed in the great flood of March 1938. In 2 miles you pass under Swan Rock, a towering wall west of the river with the outline of a giant swan etched in gray. When the canyon broadens and curves northwest, climb to your right and follow the old roadbed high above the river. In another ½ mile you turn north again, descend 100 feet and reach a highway bridge seemingly out of place. This is the famous "Bridge to Nowhere," the most imposing remnant of the East Fork Road of yesteryear. Cross the bridge and turn right, following a narrow trail that drops into the heart of The Narrows, the most impressive gorge in the Angeles. In ¼ mile, down to your right just above the tumultuous river, is unimproved Narrows Trail Camp, beckoning you to stay overnight.

Note: The area adjacent to the "Bridge to Nowhere" is private property. Some mining exploratory work is being done. Hikers are allowed to cross the bridge and continue through the upper Narrows, but please respect private property. ▲

85 East Fork, San Gabriel River— Ranger Station to The Narrows, Iron Fork, Fish Fork, Mine Gulch, Prairie Fork, Cabin Flat

HIKE LENGTH: 14 miles one way; 3200' elevation gain

CLASSIFICATION: Strenuous

SEASON: November-June

TOPO MAPS: Glendora, Crystal Lake, Mt. San Antonio

Features

This long canyon trip—best done as an overnight backpack—traverses the entire middle and upper sections of the East Fork, from the lower ranger station to Cabin Flat, where the dirt road from Blue Ridge comes down Prairie Fork. Enroute you pass through some spectacular canyon scenery and visit historic mining areas—most notably Heaton Flat, where Billy Heaton settled and mined in the 90s; Iron Fork, once the home, vegetable garden and social meeting place of miner George Trogden; and Mine Gulch, the lair of hunter-miner-mountain man Charles "Tom" Vincent. The mines are gone, but there are some inviting wilderness campsites in the upper canyon.

This trip can be done in one long day if you're in a monumental hurry, but it's much more enjoyable to stay the night at one of the four trail camps, sleeping alongside the stream under stately live oaks and, higher up, big-cone spruce. A long car shuttle is required between the East Fork Ranger Station and Cabin Flat. As an alternative—making the trip easier—you can reverse the trip and go downstream instead of up. The trip should not be done when the water is high; there are upwards of 30 stream crossings enroute.

Description

From Azusa drive up the San Gabriel Canyon Road 10 miles, then turn east on the East Fork Road and continue 8 more miles to the East Fork Ranger Station. Park just below the station.

To drive to the upper end of the traverse, proceed to Big Pines on the north side of the range, then 2 miles up the Angeles Crest to Blue Ridge. Turn left (east) onto the dirt Blue Ridge Road and follow it along the ridge and down into the upper end of Prairie Fork to Cabin Flat, 11½ miles from the Angeles Crest Highway junction.

From the East Fork Ranger Station (lower end), proceed up-canyon to The Narrows as described in Trip 84, 4½ miles to The Narrows wilderness campsite. It is about ¾ of a mile through The Narrows to Iron Fork wilderness campsite, site of Trogden's. If the water is not too high, you can hike right through The Narrows to Iron Fork. Or you can take the old P.L.&P. (Pacific Light & Power) Trail, built in 1911 when a power plant was projected below The Narrows. To reach the P.L.&P., descend into the canyon about ¼ mile south of the "Bridge to Nowhere," and pick up the footpath switchbacking up the west side of the gorge. The old trail traverses above The Narrows, then descends to Iron Fork. Either Iron Fork or Fish Fork wilderness campsite, a mile farther upstream, makes the best overnight stopover. The old trail between them, high on the west slope, is badly eroded, airy in spots and dangerous, so it is best to walk right up the riverbed unless the water is high. In fact, this section, rather than The Narrows, is the most difficult part of the trip.

"Bridge to Nowhere," Narrows, East Fork

Above Fish Fork, the canyon becomes less precipitous. The trail follows the east slope for about 2 miles, then descends to the broad streambed and continues to Mine Gulch wilderness campsite, 5 miles from Fish Fork. Here three tributaries join to form the main East Fork—Mine Gulch, Vincent Gulch and Prairie Fork. The trail turns east and ascends broad Prairie Fork, under a forest canopy of oak, spruce and pine, to the trailhead at Cabin Flat, about 3 miles from Mine Gulch.

Note: The road into Prairie Fork to Cabin Flat is not always open. Check with the Forest Service at Big Pines (619) 249-3504) before attempting this trip. ▲

86 East Fork Ranger Station to Iron Mountain

HIKE LENGTH:	15 miles round trip; 6000' elevation gain
CLASSIFICATION:	Strenuous
SEASON:	March-June
TOPO MAPS:	Glendora, Mount Baldy, Mount San Antonio

Features

8007' Iron Mountain is by far the least accessible peak in the San Gabriels. It towers as a mighty sentinel at the west end of San Antonio Ridge, standing perpetual guard over the East Fork of the San Gabriel River, whose waters rampage a mile below. No trails approach its isolated summit, and to climb it you must start miles away and thousands of feet below.

East Fork miners knew it as Sheep Mountain, for the large herds of bighorn sheep that once made their home on its rugged flanks. Today Iron Mountain is a last citadel of these "statuesque masters of the lofty crags." Easily disturbed by man, about 600 remain in the most isolated recesses of the range.

This is a long, extremely strenuous climb, the first 2500' on trail, the last 3500' up a trailless, chaparral-and-forest-covered ridge. Do it only if you are in excellent physical condition. Wear lug-soled boots and carry two full canteens. This trip can be dangerous under wintery conditions; the ridge becomes icy and footing can be slippery—definitely not recommended. Someone signing the summit register called this "The mother of all hikes," which indeed it is, at least for the San Gabriels.

Description

From Azusa, drive up San Gabriel Canyon 10 miles, then turn right (east) and follow the East Fork Road another 8 miles to the East Fork Ranger Station. Park just below the station.

Walk north along the fire road above the East Fork around two bends to the beginning of the Heaton Flat Trail, about ⅛ mile. Turn right and follow the Heaton Flat Trail east to the ridgetop, then northeast along the ridge to a 4582' saddle, 5 miles from the start. Here you leave the trail. Climb north, directly up the ridge, following a distinct path forged by climbers over the years. You reach a small saddle at 6100'. Above it you're climbing in a forest of pine and fir, a great improvement over the thorny chaparral. Continue up the ridge to the 8007' forested summit, where you will find a USGS bench mark and a register left by Sierra Club climbers.

Walk a few feet in any direction to enjoy a superb panorama, one of the best in the whole range. The peak falls sharply off in every direction except east, where broken San Antonio Ridge joins Iron Mountain to the Baldy massif. Climbers have reached Iron Mountain via this ridge, either going over the top of Mt. Baldy and traversing the entire ridge, or climbing up from Fish Fork (see Trip 88). Both of these routes are long, difficult and dangerous.

Descend the way you came. ▲

87 East Fork Ranger Station to Allison Gold Mine

HIKE LENGTH:	14 miles round trip; 3000' elevation gain
CLASSIFICATION:	Strenuous (1 day), Moderate (2 days)
SEASON:	November-June
TOPO MAPS:	Glendora, Mount Baldy, Mount San Antonio

Features

Of all man's varied activities in the San Gabriel Mountains, none has been so spectacular or so harrowing as the high-altitude lode-mining far up on the rugged slopes of the loftiest peaks in the range during the early decades of this century. The Big Horn on Mt. Baden-Powell, the Hocumac and Gold Ridge on Baldy, the Allison and Stanley Miller above the gorge of the East Fork, the Baldora, Eagle and Gold Dollar high up on San Antonio Ridge between Iron Mountain and Baldy— these were incredible feats when you consider the elevation, rugged terrain, inaccessibility, and vulnerability to the elements. Most of these gold mines had a stamp mill perched on a mountain shelf nearby, with heavy machinery for crushing ore. Lugging this machinery up near-vertical slopes and hauling out the tons of crushed ore required a high degree of fortitude and a lot of strenuous work. Of stern stuff were these mountaineering miners made!

This trip visits the rather abundant remains of the Allison Gold Mine, clinging to the precipitous slopes of Allison Gulch, high on the southwest slope of Iron Mountain. John James Allison crawled on his hands and knees through the brush to discover this mine back in 1914, and with his three sons built a cabin and a stamp mill, and gouged several tunnels out of the hard rock. The California Bureau of Mines estimates that the Allison Mine produced $50,000 in gold before it shut down in 1942. Unfortunately, the mine machinery has been vandalized and the cabins destroyed. The mine itself is in fairly good shape.

This is a rather lengthy hike, on trails that vary from fair to very poor. Unless you are a tiger, do the trip in two days, staying the night among the ghosts of the Allison miners. Carry a canteen or two; the only water is in Allison Gulch at the mine. Lug-soled boots should be worn.

The recommended return is the same way. The old trail down Allison Gulch to the East Fork is gone and should be attempted by experienced cross-country hikers only.

Description

From Azusa, drive up San Gabriel Canyon 10 miles, then turn right (east) and follow the East Fork Road another 8 miles to the locked gate just past the East Fork Ranger Station. Park off the road, taking care not to block the gate.

Walk north along the fire road above the East Fork around two bends to the beginning of the Heaton Flat Trail, hidden behind a cluster of recently planted trees, about ¼ mile. Turn right and follow the Heaton Flat Trail east to the ridgetop, then northeast along the ridge, around and over numerous bumps, to a 4582' saddle, 5 miles from the start. Just beyond the saddle, look for the old Allison Trail leading left (west) along the slope. Follow this trail, eroded and overgrown in spots (it hasn't been worked since 1942) out to the end of the ridge, then back northeast through oak and big-cone spruce, across Laurel Gulch and on around to the mine in Allison Gulch, 3 miles from the saddle.

The best camping spots are just outside the tunnel, or across the creek adjacent to the cabin remains.

Return the same way. The old trails from the Allison Mine to the Stanley Miller Mine and down Allison Gulch are in very poor condition and *not* recommended. ▲

88 Prairie Fork to Pine Mountain Ridge, Sheep Mountain Wilderness, Little Fish Fork, Upper Fish Fork

HIKE LENGTH: 9 miles round trip; 1800' gain

CLASSIFICATION: Moderate

SEASON: June-October

TOPO MAP: Mount San Antonio

Features

The rugged, rock-ribbed chasm of the Fish Fork, San Gabriel River is one of the most isolated and wild recesses in the San Gabriel Mountains. The canyon is wedged tightly between two high mountain ridges—the long hogback of Pine Mountain Ridge on the north, the sawtoothed wall of San Antonio Ridge on the south. Looming high over its head is the gray mass of Old Baldy. Melting snows from the great mountain nourish the stream that swishes and tumbles and summersaults down the chasm. Dotting the slopes and crowding the sheltered recesses are isolated stands of ponderosa pine, white fir and incense cedar, along with many stumps—the area was logged many years ago. The air is crisp with the chill of elevation.

If you like the high country to yourself, this is the trip for you. In summer, when lines of hikers tramp the more familiar trails out of Crystal Lake and San Antonio Canyon, and crawl over the summits of the Angeles Crest, walk this footpath from Pine Mountain Ridge to Fish Fork to relish the solitude and quiet beauty you find here. At trail's end in upper Fish Fork is an unimproved camping area, set in a sylvan sanctuary deep in the bowels of the canyon. You may want to spend some time here; it's one of the most isolated haunts in the Angeles.

Description

From Big Pines, drive up the Angeles Crest Highway to Blue Ridge, 2 miles. Turn left (east) onto the dirt Blue Ridge Road and follow it up and along the ridge, then down into Prairie Fork almost to Lupine Campground, 8½ miles. Just before reaching the campground, turn left and park at the beginning of the Pine Mountain Ridge Road.

Walk up the dirt road, passing the Sheep Mountain Wilderness sign, and up the dirt road to the top of Pine Mountain Ridge, then left (southeast) down and around the open slope. The old logging road ends and you follow the trail across an intervening ridge and steeply down the forested slope to Little Fish Fork and an unimproved campsite on a small bench next to the creek, 3½ miles. Just before reaching the bench is a junction: left is the trail up to Dawson Peak and the primitive Blue Ridge-Mt. Baldy Trail; the right branch drops down to Fish Fork. Go right. Your trail fords Little Fish Fork, then drops steeply to upper Fish Fork, 4½ miles from the start. There is a delightful wilderness campsite, shaded by tall pines and incense cedars, on a bench just above the rushing stream.

There is no trail up or down Fish Fork; you can follow the bubbling creek a short distance in either direction, but you soon reach

Fish Fork

rock-ribbed narrows and it is dangerous to continue very far, particularly downstream.

Return the same way—uphill most of the way back. Or, with a car shuttle, take the abandoned, somewhat eroded trail up to Dawson Peak and back to Blue Ridge—a scenic but long way around. ▲

89 Big Pines to Blue Ridge

HIKE LENGTH: 4 miles round trip; 850' elevation gain

CLASSIFICATION: Easy

SEASON: June-October

TOPO MAP: Mount San Antonio

Features

This is a very pleasant uphill walk on the north slope of Blue Ridge. Your trail starts up through stands of scrub oak, black oak, and Jeffrey pine, changing to white fir, sugar pine, and lodgepole pine as you climb over 7,000 feet. Vistas are far-reaching first north over Table Mountain to the tawny desert expanse, then, atop Blue Ridge, south into the yawning chasm of the San Gabriel River's East Fork, with Mt. Baldy, Iron Mountain, and Mt. Baden-Powell as imposing backdrops. This is a hike you should stroll rather than stride, savor rather than gulp. Go slowly and enjoy nature's delights.

Description

Drive to Big Pines, on State Highway 2 four miles west of Wrightwood on the north slope of the San Gabriels. Leave your car in the parking area on the south side of the highway, right across from the Big Pines Forest Station.

From the parking area, cross the dirt road and descend east about 50 yards to the signed trailhead. (Do not start up the dirt road.) Follow the trail as it climbs around a low ridge, drops to a trickling watercourse, then steadily climbs through open forest. You cross a dirt road and zigzag higher, with views opening to the north, over Table Mountain to the desert. After 2 miles you reach the top of Blue Ridge and a junction with Forest Road 3N06 and the Pacific Crest Trail. Right across the road is Blue Ridge Public Campground, tables, stoves, and restrooms. For the best view southward into the deep gorge of the East Fork, walk about ¼ mile up Road 3N06.

Return the way you came. You may wish to stay the night at Blue Ridge Public Campground. ▲

90 Glendora Ridge Road to Sunset Peak

HIKE LENGTH:	7 miles round trip; 1350' elevation gain
CLASSIFICATION:	Moderate
SEASON:	November-June
TOPO MAP:	Mt. Baldy

Features

In winter and early spring, when snow blankets the high peaks of the range and the air is crisp and clear, the ascent of Sunset Peak is a particularly rewarding experience. From the 5796' summit you get a grandstand vista of the great horseshoe ridge—crowned by massive Mt. Baldy—that encircles upper San Antonio Canyon. To the northwest, beyond the deep canyons of the East Fork country, looms the line of peaks above Crystal Lake.

It's an easy stroll up the 3½-mile fire road to the summit, well worth the effort to take in the high-country panorama under winter's glistening mantle.

Description

From the south end of Mt. Baldy Village, turn west up the Glendora Ridge Road. Go over Cow Canyon Saddle to the beginning of Forest Road 2N07, 4.2 miles. Park your car in the small parking area on the left, next to 2N07.

Proceed past the locked gate up 2N07. You ascend at a moderate grade through open chaparral, passing groves of Big Cone Douglas-fir and some Jeffrey Pine. In 2 miles you pass a junction with the road going down to Cow Canyon Saddle. Continue ahead, up 2N07, to a second junction at the ridgetop saddle. Make a sharp left and follow the spur road to the summit (5796').

On top, you'll find cement pillars and debris from the fire lookout tower that was once here. After taking in the splendid panorama, descend the way you came. A firebreak drops steeply down the north ridge of the mountain, but this route of descent is not recommended.

Note: The old route from Cow Canyon Saddle is now blocked by a private property owner. ▲

91

Manker Flat to Baldy Notch, Devils Backbone, Mt. San Antonio

HIKE LENGTH: 13 miles round trip; 3800′ elevation gain
CLASSIFICATION: Strenuous (moderate by taking ski lift)
SEASON: June-October
TOPO MAPS: Telegraph Peak, Mount San Antonio

Features

St. Anthony of Padua, a 13th century Franciscan priest and worker of miracles, is well represented in Southern California. His name crowns the San Gabriel Mountains—Mount San Antonio. Legend has it that the title was bestowed by the padres of Mission San Gabriel in the 1790s. Early American miners, digging in upper San Antonio Canyon in the 1870s, dubbed the peak a more earthy "Old Baldy," for its barren, roundish summit. Although the U.S. Board on Geographic Names has decreed "Mount San Antonio" as official, "Old Baldy" or "Mt. Baldy" is still the favorite of most sightseers and hikers today.

Massive Mount San Antonio—or Old Baldy if you prefer—is the grand climax of the 50-mile backbone of the San Gabriels. No other peak in the range rises to challenge its 10,064′ elevation. From its summit you look over a good part of Southern California—an expense of mountain, desert and coastal lowland. On those rare days when haze does not muddy the atmosphere, the hiker on its boulder-strewn top can make out the tawny ramparts of the southern High Sierra, 160 miles distant.

Old Baldy is a huge mountain, by Southern California standards. Its sprawling gray bulk overwhelms lesser summits and makes up for any lack of sharp relief. Long descending ridges and broad slopes of disintegrating granitic rock drop far down into shadowy canyons. Among the folds of its granite robes are sylvan dells where sparkling streams and waterfalls rush downward, and ferns grow lush in the shade of pine and cedar. Its higher slopes are dotted with lodgepole and limber pine: Some stand tall and erect, proud sentinels of the ridgetops; others, bent and gnarled by nature's high-altitude fury, form grotesque shapes. All contribute to the elegance, order and beauty of the alpine landscape.

Who it was that made the first ascent of Mt. San Antonio will probably never be known. Serrano Indians, who knew the great mountain as "Joat," their word for snow, crossed the San Antonio-Lytle Creek Divide (Baldy Notch) centuries before the arrival of the white man, and may have walked the short distance to the top, although Indians of that day appear to have had little interest in "conquering" mountain peaks. Perhaps an early miner at the Banks (later Hocumac) Mine just below Baldy Notch scrambled to the summit. The earliest ascent on record was made by Louis Nell and a party of soldiers from the U.S. Army's Wheeler Survey on July 1, 1875.

The first name associated with the peak was that of William B. Dewey, who made the ascent in 1882. Dewey reported seeing no human trail up Baldy, but bears were plentiful and many bear trails contoured the higher slopes of the mountain. Dewey spent most of his life in San Antonio Canyon. In 1886-87-88 he served as a mountain guide for Stoddard's Resort, leading many persons to the summit and back. In the summers of 1910-11-12 he built and managed with Mrs. Dewey the "Baldy Summit Inn," a mere 80' below the top, the most unique resort in the west. It consisted of two small stone buildings and several tents securely anchored against a wind that sometimes reached gale force. Saddle horses and mules brought guests up from Camp Baldy (today's Mt. Baldy Village) every day. Fire destroyed most of the camp in 1913, and Dewey never rebuilt it. Dewey made a total of 133 ascents of Mt. San Antonio, probably a record even today. The last was in 1936, when he was 71 years old.

Old Baldy is a hiker's delight. The trail is well beaten and easy-graded (except the summit pitch), the thin air is invigorating, and vistas are breathtaking almost the entire distance. During summer and fall weekends, thousands of people, young and old alike, make the ascent. Probably no other western mountain not reached by road is climbed by so many people.

West Baldy

Description

Drive to almost the upper end of Mt. Baldy Road, 15 miles from Claremont. Park on the left (west) side of the divided road ½ mile *below* the ski-lift parking area, adjacent to the locked gate of the Baldy fire road.

Walk past the locked gate and up the dirt road as it winds around the ridge for a good view of San Antonio Falls, then climbs northward, with switchbacks near the top, to Baldy Notch and the top of the ski lift.

From Baldy Notch, follow the broad path east 150 yards to "Desert View" and a wooden sign pointing left (northwest) toward Mt. Baldy. Turn left and proceed up the fire road, switchbacking up a broad slope shaded by Jeffrey and sugar pine, white fir, and incense cedar. The fire road ends at the top of a ski lift just before the razorback ridge known, with good reason, as the Devils Backbone. The trail proceeds along the backbone—people have slipped here, take care—climbs around the south slope of "Little Baldy" through a thinning forest of lodgepole, emerges from the trees, and reaches a wind-battered saddle. From here the trail steepens considerably as it ascends nearly bare slopes the final 400', here and there passing a few stunted limber pines. The top is a gently tapered expanse of boulders, barren of vegetation, commanding the broadest panorama in the San Gabriel Mountains.

Return the way you came. An alternative to make the trip 6 miles with 1300 feet less elevation gain is to utilize the ski lift, usually open on summer weekends, for $6 per round trip. ▲

92 Mt. Baldy Village to Mt. San Antonio and Baldy Notch

HIKE LENGTH: 14 miles; 6000' elevation gain
CLASSIFICATION: Strenuous
SEASON: June-October
TOPO MAPS: Mt. Baldy, Mount San Antonio, Telegraph Peak

Features

The great south ridge of Baldy rises in continuous welts from Cow Canyon Saddle to the summit, gaining more than 6000' elevation in 3 horizontal miles. The ridge begins in dense chaparral, passes through belts of Jeffrey and sugar pine, white fir and lodgepole pine, and terminates above timberline. Following the crest of this ridge most of the way, the Bear Flat, or Old Mt. Baldy, Trail is one of the most strenuous hikes in the San Gabriels. Its 6000' of elevation gain from Mt. Baldy Village to the top is the most of any footpath in the range.

This is the hard way to do Old Baldy, and is only for those in excellent physical condition. Veteran hikers call this a "no nonsense" trail—direct, uphill all the way, in some spots unbelievably steep. Those who complete this all-day trip are guaranteed to be "pooped" at the finish.

Years ago, this was the main trail up Baldy. It was built in 1889 by Dr. B. H. Fairchild of Claremont and Fred Deli of Deli's Camp in San Antonio Canyon. The men envisioned a great astronomical observatory on the summit, but it was never built. In ensuing years parties from Camp Baldy (today's Mt. Baldy Village) would go up the trail on foot or horseback, watch the glorious sunset from the top, and stay the night at William B. Dewey's "Baldy Summit Inn" (see Trip 91), returning the next day. With the extension of the road to the head of San Antonio Canyon and the construction of the Devils Backbone Trail by the CCC in 1935-36, the old Bear Flat route fell into disuse. Few use it nowadays (for obvious reason!), although it remains easy to follow if you are physically—and temperamentally—so inclined.

Description

A car shuttle is necessary. Drive one car to the ski-lift parking area, 15 miles from Claremont. Return to Mt. Baldy Village with the other car and park on Bear Canyon Road, about 100 yards south of the new Mt. Baldy Road, about 100 yards south of the Forest Service's new Mt. Baldy Visitor Center. The largest parking area is at the bottom of Bear Canyon Road, on your right. These is a small parking area about 200 yards up the road. Non-residents are not permitted to drive farther, but hikers are welcome.

Proceed on foot up Bear Canyon Road. The end of the road is reached in ½ mile, where a wooden sign points to the Bear Flat-Mount Baldy Trail. The trail switchbacks up slopes shaded by live oak and spruce to Bear Flat, a small mountain meadow clothed in a carpet of lush grass, 1½ miles. Here is the last water enroute, so fill both of your canteens. Above Bear Flat, the trail zigzags very steeply up through shadeless chaparral, the most unpleasant part of the trip on a hot day, to the crest of the south ridge. Here, amid cool stands of pine and fir, the view opens to the west, across the deep canyons of the San Gabriel watershed to the Mt. Wilson-Strawberry Peak-Charlton Flat country. The trail now ascends the ridge line, over an extremely steep and loose-footed pitch, known in the old days as "Hardscrabble," to "The Narrows," a razorback saddle at 9200'. After crossing the bare saddle, the route enters an open forest of weather-toughened lodgepole pine, traverses the east slope of West Baldy, emerges above timberline, and climbs finally to the 10,064' summit for a top-of-the-world vista.

The descent is via the Devils Backbone (see Trip 91) to Baldy Notch, then down either the ski lift or the zigzagging fire road to the roadhead.

A satisfying but most exhausting day's walk! ▲

93 Manker Flat to Upper San Antonio Creek, Baldy Bowl, Mt. San Antonio

HIKE LENGTH: 9 miles round trip; 3800' elevation gain

CLASSIFICATION: Strenuous

SEASON: June-October

TOPO MAP: Mount San Antonio

Features

This is the most direct way to Mt. Baldy's summit, but also the steepest. It's trail all the way, but some sections of the footpath, particularly from Baldy Bowl to the top, are loose and not well maintained. Nevertheless, this is one of the most scenic and historical hikes in the San Gabriels. You pass near the remains of the old Gold Ridge Mine, worked in the 1890s; the Sierra Club's San Antonio Ski Hut; Baldy Bowl, where Southern California skiing was born in the 1930s; and, near the top, the site of Baldy Summit Inn, once the highest trail resort in the range.

Be in good physical condition, wear lug-soled boots, and tote plenty of water—the only sure source is a small stream you cross at the edge of Baldy Bowl, and even this may disappear by summer's end in years of below-average rainfall.

Description

The hike begins at the gated access road to Baldy Notch, ½ mile below the ski-lift parking area (same as Trip 91). Be sure not to block access to the gate.

Walk past the locked gate and up the dirt road, passing a fine view of San Antonio Falls at the first switchback. About ⅓ mile beyond the switchback, look for the Ski Hut Trail that begins steeply on your left. (There is no sign here, so look carefully.) The trail climbs at a steady steep grade up the east slope of upper San Antonio Canyon, through an open forest of Jeffrey and then lodgepole pine. On a sloping bench to your left, 1¼ miles up and about 100 yards off the trail, are the stone foundations of the Gold Ridge Mine, worked in the years 1897 to about 1904. Another steep ½ mile gets you to the lower edge of Baldy Bowl. To your right, 50 feet away, is the Sierra Club's San Antonio Ski Hut, built in 1935, burned in 1936, and rebuilt in 1937. You go left as your trail drops down to the trickling headwaters of San Antonio Creek, the only sure water en route. The water is icy-cold and delicious, but it should be purified before drinking (as should all water in the San Gabriels). The trail, much less distinct now, contours across the lower edge of Baldy Bowl, a skiers' delight in winter. Watch your step here; some of the boulders are loose. Beyond, you re-enter the lodgepole forest and zigzag very steeply up to Mt. Baldy's great southeast ridge. Your footpath ascends the ridgeline, passes just left of some small rock gendarmes, reaches the site of William Dewey's Baldy Summit Inn (open for hardy guests during the summers of 1910 to 1913), and finally arrives on the broad, barren summit of Mt. San Antonio (10,064'), 4½ steep miles from the start.

Return the same way. Or, with 2½ miles more walking but much easier going, descend via the Devils Backbone and Baldy Notch (see Trip 91). ▲

94 Stockton Flat to Baldy Notch

HIKE LENGTH: 8 miles round trip; 2000' elevation gain
CLASSIFICATION: Moderate
SEASON: June-October
TOPO MAP: Telegraph Peak

Features

Stockton Flat lies at the head of Lytle Creek, in a sloping bowl ringed by lofty peaks and ridges. This is the backyard of the San Antonio country, close under the gray mantle of Old Baldy itself. In the shadow of the massive mountain, snow lingers longer than in other parts of the range, providing coolness and moisture for handsome stands of pine and fir.

The flat was named for W. H. Stockton, who filed a timber claim here back in the 1880s. But apparently he did no cutting and never received a patent, and the flat reverted to the National Forest. The public campground on the forested flat there has been dismantled.

A steep dirt road, built originally in the '90s to provide access to the Hocumac gold mine just over the ridge from Baldy Notch, climbs up the backside of the Baldy-Telegraph Ridge to the notch. This hiking trip take s you up this old mountain byway and offers you a number of options. It's a pleasant summer outing, when the air is crisp but not biting, and the open forest offers both shade and sunshine.

Description

From Interstate 15, 16 miles east of Ontario, take the Sierra Ave. offramp. Go left (north) and follow Lytle Creek Road to Lytle Creek Village, 9½ miles. Above the village the road turns to dirt and continues to Stockton Flat, 7 more miles. There are several bad spots that could pose a problem for low-slung standard vehicles. Park outside the locked gate on Stockton Flat.

From the flat, walk up the poor dirt road, going left (south) at a junction, and wind steeply up the mountainside above Coldwater Canyon. As you gain elevation, vistas open up to the north and east, across the Lytle Creek and Cajon Pass country. Notice the parallel northwest-southeast orientation of the topography, following the line of California's greatest earthquake fault, the San Andreas. Finally, there is one long switchback, and you round the head of Coldwater Canyon's north fork to Baldy Notch, about 4 miles from the start.

Now you have several options. You can visit the Notch Restaurant, then return the way you came. You can take the Devils Backbone Trail to Baldy's summit (see Trip 91). You can take the trail south over the 3 "T"s—Thunder, Telegraph and Timber—to Icehouse Saddle, where more options open up (see Trip 95). Or, if you can arrange to be picked up in San Antonio Canyon, you can take the ski lift or hike down the fire road to Manker Flat, where you meet the paved road.

This trip offers a different approach to the Mt. Baldy country, one that few of the multitude of Baldy hikers ever attempt. ▲

95 Baldy Notch to Thunder, Telegraph, Timber Mtns., Icehouse Saddle, Icehouse Canyon

HIKE LENGTH: 8½ miles: 2700' elevation gain; 3400' loss
CLASSIFICATION: Strenuous
SEASON: June-October
TOPO MAPS: Telegraph Peak, Cucamonga Peak, Mt. Baldy

Features

Between Baldy Notch and Icehouse Saddle, at the head of the great horseshoe ridge that encircles upper San Antonio Canyon, are three summits rising over 8000'—Thunder Mountain (8587'), Telegraph Peak (8985') and Timber Mountain (8303'). Mountaineers know these forested knobs as "The 3 T's." This trip traverses over *or* around these three summits—depending on whether or not you are a peak-bagger—on good trail.

This is ideal summer hiking country. The well-beaten ridge trail zigzags over crests and across saddles, through open stands of pine, fir and cedar, offering continuous vistas. Snow patches linger in sheltered

Folded metamorphic rock, Upper Icehouse Canyon

recesses well into the warmer months. The high mountain air is cool, clear and clean, with seldom a trace of urban-generated murkiness that clogs lungs at lower elevations. From Telegraph Peak, the climax of the trip, the desert view rivals the one from Baldy. (Telegraph's name dates from the 1890s, when government surveyors installed a heliograph on the summit and signaled to cohorts on Mt. Wilson, 22 airline miles away.)

This trip requires a car shuttle and covers a lot of high country, but you get a head start by utilizing the ski lift to Baldy Notch. From there it's 1100' up Telegraph, then downhill most of the rest of the way to Icehouse Canyon parking area. For this reason it is classified as "moderate." If you want to do it the other way, add almost 2000' more climbing and consider it "strenuous."

Description

Drive to Icehouse Canyon parking area, 1½ miles above Mt. Baldy Village, and leave one car. Drive your other car to the ski-lift parking lot at the upper end of San Antonio Canyon road, 15 miles from Claremont.

Ride the ski lift to Baldy Notch (operated weekends and holidays all year). An alternate way to the Notch, one which adds 3½ miles and 1500' gain to the hike, is to walk the fire road from just below the lower end of the ski-lift parking area, passing San Antonio Falls.

From Baldy Notch Restaurant, walk east about 150 yards to "Desert View," where you pick up the fire road leading southeast up Gold Ridge. Follow the fire road to Thunder Mountain, the top of the highest ski lift, 1 ½ miles. From the end of the dirt road, follow the trail as it traverses and climbs around the south ridge of Thunder Mountain, then drops 500' to a saddle. From here the trail switchbacks steeply 800' to the top of Telegraph Peak ridge. Turn left (northeast) and follow the ridgetop ⅛ mile to the summit, 3 miles from Baldy Notch. Return to the main trail and follow it south along the ridge—downhill except where you climb briefly around the west slope of Timber Mountain—to Icehouse Saddle, two miles. Then turn right (west) and descend the Icehouse Canyon Trail (see Trip 96) to Icehouse Canyon parking area. ▲

96 Icehouse Canyon to Icehouse Saddle

HIKE LENGTH: 8 miles round trip; 2600' elevation gain

CLASSIFICATION: Moderate

SEASON: June-October

TOPO MAPS: Mt. Baldy, Cucamonga Peak

Features

Icehouse Canyon is the hikers' gateway to the eastern high country and the Cucamonga Wilderness. Its broad, V-shaped portal leads east from San Antonio Canyon, 1 ½ miles north of Mt. Baldy Village, and climbs 2600' to Icehouse Saddle, a prominent gap on the great Telegraph-Ontario Ridge. The saddle is a major trail junction, with routes leading in four directions.

For hikers of moderate ability, the trip up-canyon to Icehouse Saddle is rewarding. You pass through some of the finest stands of incense cedar in the range, and the ponderosa and sugar pines are healthy and towering. From the saddle you look into the inviting Cucamonga Wilderness country and down over the Lytle Creek drainage.

Legend has it that the magnificent cedar beams for Mission San Gabriel were cut in the canyon, then laboriously dragged down to the lowland by oxen teams. For years it was known as Cedar Canyon (now the name for a tributary of Icehouse Canyon). The present name dates from the 1860s, when an ice plant in the lower canyon supplied ice to valley residents.

The lower reaches of the canyon are dotted with private cabins. Once there were many more; the big flood of 1938 wreaked havoc here, as it did in other canyons of the range. Today, the boulder-strewn floor of Icehouse Canyon bears testimony to nature's torrential fury.

Description

Drive to Icehouse Canyon parking area, 1½ miles above Mt. Baldy Village just off Mt. Baldy Road.

Walk up the trail that starts just to the right of the parking area. In the first 1½ miles you pass many private cabins, climbing gently through a forest of oak, big-cone spruce, and incense cedar. You reach a junction. To your left is the Chapman Trail, which climbs in gentle switchbacks to Cedar Glen, 1 mile, and continues on an airy "high route" along the precipitous north slope of the canyon to a junction with the main Icehouse Canyon Trail, 5 miles from the start. At the before-mentioned junction, the main trail continues straight ahead, passes a cluster of cabins, follows the creek another ½ mile, then crosses it. The creek disappears as you climb steadily, under an open forest of pine and incense cedar and enter Cucamonga Wilderness, marked with a large wooden sign. In 3 miles you reach Columbine Spring, a small seepage of icy-cold water just below the trail. This is the last water enroute. Beyond, the trail switchbacks up under a shady canopy of tall pines and firs, passes a junction with the upper end of the Chapman Trail, and reaches Icehouse Saddle, 4 miles from the start.

You can take a good look, then return the way you came. You can turn left (north) and follow the trail that climbs around the west slope of Timber Mountain and over Telegraph Peak, then drops to Baldy Notch (see Trip 95). You can turn hard right (southwest) and take the lateral trail to Kellys Camp and Ontario Peak (see Trip 97). You can go right (southeast) on the trail that contours around the east slopes of Bighorn Peak to Cucamonga Saddle, then climb the north face of Cucamonga Peak (see Trip 98). Or you can drop eastward down the Middle Fork Trail to Lytle Creek (see Trip 99).

Whichever option you take, you are sure to travel through some of the finest high country in the range.

Buy your Forest Adventure Permit at the Mt. Baldy Visitor Center before starting your hike. Cars not showing permit will be ticketed and owner fined. ▲

97 Icehouse Canyon to Icehouse Saddle, Kellys Camp, Ontario Peak

HIKE LENGTH: 13 miles round trip; 3600' elevation gain

CLASSIFICATION: Moderate to Strenuous

SEASON: June-October

TOPO MAPS: Mt. Baldy, Cucamonga Peak

Features

From Icehouse Saddle the long, multi-humped Ontario Ridge juts southwestward, standing above 8000' for some 2 miles, separating the San Antonio from the Cucamonga watershed. Blanketing the upper north slopes of the ridge is a lush forest—rather dense in sheltered recesses, thinning out on the crests-of white fir, ponderosa and sugar pine and, higher up, lodgepole pine.

Betty Dessert

Baldy from Icehouse Canyon Trail

The Ontario Peak Trail traverses this ridge, staying just on the north side of the crest, from Icehouse Saddle to the 8693' summit. Enroute it visits Kellys Camp—established as a mining prospect by John Kelly in 1905, turned into a trail resort by Henry Delker in 1922, and now an unimproved wilderness campsite and one of the best in the eastern high country.

You can do this trip in one day as a rather strenuous up-and-back hike, or you can make it a more leisurely outing by staying the night at Kellys Camp. If camping overnight you can use the cabin foundations or sack out under the pines. A large campfire ring bespeaks the frequent presence of Boy Scout groups. Just beyond the camp is a small spring, flowing in early season, but sometimes drying up in late summer and fall. If it's been a dry year, better pack your own water.

Description

Drive to Icehouse Canyon parking area, 1½ miles above Mt. Baldy Village just off Mt. Baldy Road.

Walk up the trail to Icehouse Saddle (see Trip 96). From the saddle, take the far-right fork, traveling southwest across the forested slopes. A mile of level and uphill walking through the forest brings you to Kelly's Camp. Your trail climbs around the left side of the wilderness campsite, then circles right and climbs to the top of the ridge, intersects the short lateral trail leading left to Bighorn Peak, and turns west. You walk through a lodgepole forest, much of it burned in a 1980 fire, passing just to the right of two false summits, and finally surmount Ontario Peak, 2½ miles from Icehouse Saddle.

Enjoy the superb view from the top, then return the same way. ▲

98 Icehouse Canyon to Icehouse Saddle, Cucamonga Wilderness, Cucamonga Peak

HIKE LENGTH:	12 miles round trip; 3800' elevation gain
CLASSIFICATION:	Strenuous
SEASON:	June-October
TOPO MAPS:	Mt. Baldy, Cucamonga Peak

Features

The Cucamonga Wilderness, enlarged to its present 12,781 acres when Congress passed the California Wilderness Act in 1984, is a high subalpine region of 8000' peaks and deep canyons-pine-forested, precipitous and relatively isolated. This superb, nearly pristine high country extends from upper Icehouse Canyon and Thunder Mountain ridge eastward some 4 miles to Grizzly Ridge, the upper Middle Fork of Lytle Creek, and rugged Cucamonga Peak. It is the only wilderness in Southern California that encompasses parts of two national forests—Angeles and San Bernardino.

8859' Cucamonga Peak is the eastern citadel of the range. Its steep battlements rise abruptly from Cucamonga Saddle on one side and San Sevaine Ridge on the other, offering nothing but discouragement to faint-of-heart and out-of-condition hikers.

The only easy access to Cucamonga Peak and its surrounding wilderness is via Icehouse Canyon and Saddle. A well-marked trail contours around the east slope of Bighorn Peak and zigzags steeply up the north side of Cucamonga. It's a long hike, but the view from the summit, taking in the eastern end of the range, the San Bernardino Valley and the mountains beyond, is well worth the effort.

Description

Drive to Icehouse Canyon parking area, 1½ miles above Mt. Baldy Village, just off Mt. Baldy Road.

Walk up the trail to Icehouse Saddle (see Trip 96). From the saddle turn right (southeast), passing trails to Ontario Peak (right) and Middle Fork Lytle Creek (left), and follow the trail as it contours through open stands of ponderosa pine and white fir around the east slopes of Bighorn Peak and gains Cucamonga Saddle. Here you can look down into the wild, trailless gorge of Cucamonga Canyon. The trail then switchbacks steeply up the north face of Cucamonga Peak to within 200' of the summit and then turns east. The easiest way to the top is to stay on the trail until it gains the east ridge, then double back up the crest.

Return the same way.

With a long car shuttle you can descend the trail eastward to San Sevaine Flats (see Trip 100). ▲

99 Middle Fork of Lytle Creek to Cucamonga Wilderness, Icehouse Saddle

HIKE LENGTH: 12 miles round trip; 3600' elevation gain

CLASSIFICATION: Strenuous (1 day), Moderate (2 days)

SEASON: June-October

TOPO MAPS: Telegraph Peak, Cucamonga Peak

Features

The 8500-acre Cucamonga Wilderness covers the eastern end of the San Antonio high country, where the mountains are abruptly cut off by the earth-grinding cleaver of the San Andreas Fault. The terrain is as steep and rugged as any in the range. Razorback ridges and broken battlements of grayish, decomposing granite plunge downward from Telegraph and Cucamonga peaks to meet the strange slanting valleys of the great earthquake fault.

This trip takes the eastern approach to the Wilderness, climbing up the Middle Fork of Lytle Creek through the heart of the wild area to Icehouse Saddle on its western boundary. The trail is good and these are three wilderness campsites (formerly trail camps) for overnight stay—Stone House, Third Crossing and Comanche. You start in a semi-arid chaparral, progress upward through belts of big-cone spruce and Jeffrey pine, and end up in the cool high country of lodgepole pine and white fir. From Icehouse Saddle, one of the major trail junctions in the range, you are presented with numerous options.

You stand a good chance of having the canyon all to yourself—99% of hikers who enter the Wilderness do so from the more gentle western side, via Icehouse Canyon or Baldy Notch. If you're lucky, you may spot a timid member of the Cucamonga Herd of Nelson bighorn sheep—once plentiful but now rare in these mountains. This is one of the few islands of subalpine wilderness left in Southern California—explore it, enjoy it and protect it.

Description

From Interstate 15, 16 miles east of Ontario, take the Sierra Ave. offramp. Go left (north) and follow Lytle Creek Road to its intersection with Middle Fork Road, 2 miles past the ranger station (where you must stop for a Wilderness permit), 7½ miles from the freeway. Follow the dirt road 3 miles to the beginning of the Middle Fork Trail, marked by a wooden sign, at the road's end, and park.

Walk up the trail as it climbs the north slope above the streambed. In ½ mile you round a point and reach a trail junction. Go right, staying high on the slope; the left branch descends to the creek and Stone House wilderness campsite. You pass through stands of live oak and spruce, cross a rocky side gully, and in 2 miles reach Third Crossing wilderness campsite, a sylvan sanctuary along the stream with space for many hikers. Above Third Crossing your trail fords the creek and zigzags steeply up the slope before leveling off above the gorge of the Middle Fork's south branch. In 1½ miles you reach Comanche wilderness campsite, alongside the creek, shaded by oak, alder, cedar and fir. Above Comanche the trail follows the canyon a short distance, then climbs steeply west to Icehouse Saddle, 2 more miles.

You have numerous options from Icehouse Saddle. You can return the way you came. You can take the trail west to Kellys Camp and Ontario Peak (see Trip 97). You can go south on the Cucamonga Peak Trail (see Trip 98). You can go north over the "3 T's" (see Trip 95). Or you can descend Icehouse Canyon to Mt. Baldy Road (see Trip 96); this will require a long car shuttle. ▲

100 San Sevaine Flats to Cucamonga Peak

HIKE LENGTH: 12 miles round trip; 3300' elevation gain

CLASSIFICATION: Strenuous (1 day), Moderate (2 days)

SEASON: May-October

TOPO MAPS: Devore, Cucamonga Peak

Features

East from Cucamonga Peak, the crest of the San Gabriels drops some 3,000 feet, then continues as a gently rolling plateau for 6 miles before dropping steeply to a termination at the mouth of Lytle Creek. This east-end country is pleasant and inviting, covered largely with chaparral, plus groves of oak, spruce, cedar and pine scattered here and there in little flats and gullies. The largest of these forested glens is San Sevaine Flats, named for French winemaker Pierre Sainsevain, who tapped the springs here for his vineyards in the valley below in the 1870s. (A careless government mapmaker corrupted the name from French to Spanish at the turn of the century.) Higher up, just before the crest juts upward to Cucamonga Peak was the Joe Elliott tree, a mammoth sugar pine 7 feet 6 inches in diameter, believed to have been the largest conifer in southern California. The tree, named in honor of a former San Bernardino National Forest supervisor, fell several years ago.

This east-end country is little visited by hikers. Forest Road 1N34 up to San Sevaine Flats is usually closed; if the gate is locked, check with the Lytle Creek Ranger Station, 2½ miles farther up Lytle Creek Road.

Description

For Interstate 15, 16 miles east of Ontario, take the Sierra Avenue off-ramp. Go left (north) and follow Lytle Creek Road 1½ miles to a junction with Forest Road 1N34. Turn left and follow the latter as it twists and winds its way up the ridge to San Sevaine Flats, 5 miles. A side road right leads to San Sevaine Spring, 200 yards, the only sure water on the trip.

Just beyond San Sevaine Flats the dirt road climbs steeply up the ridge—end of the line for most standard cars. Park at one of several clearings alongside the road and begin your hike. If you have a VW, high-clearance or 4-wheel-drive vehicle, you can drive on. Follow the road as it climbs the side of the open ridge, with far-ranging views southward and ahead to the massive bulk of Cucamonga Peak, then drops into a forested recess and reaches a junction 2½ miles from San Sevaine Flats. To your right, about 50 yards, was the Joe Elliott Tree,

San Sevaine Flats

once the largest conifer in Southern California. About ¼ mile farther up the road are campsites. At the campsite the road steepens and soon ends—the absolute limit of travel for any type of vehicle.

From road's end, follow the trail as it ascends the forested gully, then switchbacks up the left (west) slope. In less than a mile you pass a large CUCAMONGA WILDERNESS Sign, then climb to a boulder-filled gully (usually dry). Your path crosses the gully and turns north, climbing to a forested ridgetop where you pass the small cabin of the "Blew Light Mine." The trail climbs steadily westward, enters a forest of lodgepole pines, rounds the ridge and turns southwest. You pass 200' under the summit of Etiwanda Peak (8662') and, ¾ mile farther, 200' under Cucamonga Peak. As your trail turns northwest, leave it and scramble through open forest to the summit (8859').

Return the same way. With a long car shuttle, you can descend the trail westward to Icehouse Canyon (see Trip 98). ▲

Appendix I:
Organized Trail Systems

Silver Moccasin Trail

For Boy Scouts in Southern California, there are few scouting challenges greater than making the "Silver Moccasin" hike across the heart of the San Gabriel Mountains. The grueling trip was first organized and mapped out by the Los Angeles Area Council of the Boy Scouts of America in 1942. The 53-mile, five-day pilgrimage begins at Chantry Flats, ascends Big Santa Anita Canyon to Newcomb Pass, drops into the West Fork of the San Gabriel River, climbs Shortcut Canyon, crosses the head of Big Tujunga to Charlton Flat, and continues its up-and-down route to Chilao. From here, it closely parallels the Angeles Crest Highway over Cloudburst Summit, down Cooper Canyon and up Little Rock Creek, over the shoulder of Mt. Williamson to Islip Saddle, and across the middle high country to climax at the Boy Scout Monument on Mt. Baden-Powell, then down to Vincent Gap, where the hike ends. The entire trip is on good trail—shown in red on the Forest Service's map of Angeles National Forest. Recommended overnight stays enroute are at West Fork Campground, Chilao Campground, Cooper Canyon Trail Camp, and Little Jimmy Trail Camp. Scouts who complete the long ramble receive the coveted Silver Moccasin award.

Pacific Crest Trail

Traversing the crest of the Pacific states from Mexico to Canada, nine tenths of its 2500 miles complete, is the Pacific Crest Trail, the most ambitious footpath in the United States. The proposal to carve this wilderness path from border to border was conceived by Clinton C. Clarke of Pasadena in 1932. He urged the Forest Service and the National Park system to knit together and extend the threads of high-country footpaths already existing, such as the Oregon Skyline Trail and California's John Muir Trail. Clarke achieved partial success before his death in 1957; he prevailed upon the Forest Service to call the footpaths in Oregon and Washington by the collective name "Pacific Crest Trail System." But not until 1968, when Congress, responding to pressure from outdoorsmen, created the Pacific Crest Trail as a national scenic trail, did active work begin to join together a border-to-border system. Many sections of the trail, particularly in Southern California, remain to be built.

In 1977 the last sections of the Pacific Crest Trail through the San Gabriels were completed. Some of the sections—particularly from Mill Creek summit west to Mt. Gleason or east to Pacifico Mountain—make excellent day hikes now detailed in this guidebook. For a full description of the trail, see Wilderness Press' *Pacific Crest Trail, Volume I· California*, by Schaffer, Schifrin, Winnett and Jenkins.

In brief outline, the PCT route through the San Gabriels, east to west, goes as follows: From Interstate 15 south of Cajon Pass up Lone Pine Canyon, across Blue Ridge to Vincent Gap, up the north slope of Mt. Baden-Powell, along the Baden-Powell-Throop ridge past Little Jimmy Campground to Islip Saddle, across the south face of Mt. Williamson, down Little Rock Creek, up Cooper Canyon to Cloudburst Summit, across the north slope of Pacifico Mountain, down to Mill Creek Summit, over Mount Gleason, to Messenger Flats, and down to Agua Dulce.

Appendix II:
Trails That Used To Be

During the Great Hiking Era (approx. 1895-1938), outdoor enthusiasts by the thousands tramped through the San Gabriels. With the building of the Angeles Crest Highway and other paved roads into the mountains, hiking interest declined, and many of these old pathways fell into disuse and disappeared. Others, not preempted by highway, are still in use today.

Below are listed some of the historic trails of yesteryear that have vanished or become virtually impassable.

Tom Sloan Trail: From its construction in 1923 until the demise of Mount Lowe Tavern in 1936, this route joining the Tavern with Switzer's in the Arroyo Seco was a busy thoroughfare. Today only parts of the trail are passable. The stretch between the Tavern and Tom Sloan Saddle is completely overgrown. The Bear Canyon link is badly eroded by water in many places. Only the last section from the middle Arroyo Seco to Commodore Switzer Trail Camp is in good shape.

Mount Lowe "8": In 1893 Professor T.S.C. Lowe financed the construction of a network of riding and hiking trails from his recently built White City on Echo Mountain. Most popular was the "Mount Lowe 8," via which a traveler could ascend and descend Mt. Lowe following a double loop route, recrossing his path just once—near Inspiration Point. Today, part of the "8" is still good trail, and part is eroded and overgrown. The readily passable sections are Castle Canyon and Mt. Lowe "East" Trails; passable but partly overgrown is the Sunset Trail from Echo Mountain to near Inspiration Point; and badly overgrown is the Mount Lowe "West" path.

Lone Tree Trail: Lowe built this steep trail from Rubio Pavilion up the divide between Rubio and Eaton Canyons to Inspiration Point in the 1890s-so named because only one pine tree was passed enroute. Today the trail is unmaintained although passable, but difficult to locate. The lower part into Rubio Canyon is completely gone; the lower terminus is now on the fire road above the Rubio Canyon water works.

Cliff Trail: This footpath between Mt. Wilson and Mt. Lowe Tavern was built in 1919, and for many years the stretch that crossed the south face of San Gabriel Peak was considered the most harrowing in the range. A misstep would send a hiker plunging 200 feet straight down. In 1942 the Mt. Lowe fire road was blasted across the face, with a tunnel bypassing the sheer part. Hikers walking the fire road today, between Eaton and Markham saddles, can see the remains of the old Cliff Trail and its handrails traversing the rock face outside the tunnel.

Eaton Canyon Trail: No other canyon in the front range of the San Gabriels can compare with Eaton in ruggedness and inaccessibility. Access into the canyon now is from above, via the Idlehour Trail. Years ago there was a cliffhanging footpath up the canyon from Eaton Falls near the canyon entrance to Camp Idlehour. Many hikers were injured in falls from this precipitous trail. Today the high fence of the Pasadena Water Department forbids entrance into the lower canyon, and the old path is closed to the public.

Sturtevant Trail: This once heavily trod footpath from Sierra Madre over the ridge into Big Santa Anita and along the west slope to Sturtevant's Camp is gone except for the middle stretch between Chantry Flat and Hoegee Trail Camp. The lower part, made obsolete by the construction of the Chantry Flat road in 1935, is eroded and blocked at both ends. The upper third from Hoegee's over the ridge to Sturtevant was passable until about 1960, but is now so badly overgrown as to be virtually nonexistent.

Monrovia Peak Trail: This was once a favorite of Big Santa Anita Canyon hikers, going from Fern Lodge up the East Fork to Clamshell Ridge and on to the Summit. Today the middle stretch from the East Fork up to the Clamshell fire road is completely overgrown and impassable.

Deer Park-Monrovia Trail: Ben Overturff built this trail from Deer Park Lodge up the long southeast ridge of Monrovia Peak to the summit in 1914-1915. It fell into disrepair when Deer Park was abandoned after the 1938 flood.

Colby Trail: Author Charles Francis Saunders once called Colby Ranch, the hospitable home of Delos, Lillian, and Nellie Colby, "the little Canaan of the Sierra Madre." From the 1890s into the 19209, this was one of the best-loved trail resorts in the range. The trail from Switzer's over Strawberry-Josephine Saddle to Colby's, built by "Pa" Colby himself, was trod by hundreds every weekend. Today the trail is passable though bushy, except for the last ½ mile into Strawberry Potrero. The Forest Service is considering reopening it.

Loomis Ranch Trail: Like Colby's, Loomis Ranch was beloved by hikers during the Great Hiking Era. This alder-shaded home of Captain Lester Loomis and his wife Grace, on Alder Creek west of Chilao, was the most remote of the trail resorts, but the popularity of Mrs. Loomis' chicken dinners and apple dumplings kept it well attended by visitors. Today Loomis Ranch is inaccessible to the public, and the old ranch trails up Alder Creek from Big Tujunga and down from Chilao are closed off.

Sierra Madre and Antelope Valley Toll Trail: See Trip 46 (p. 96).

Angeles Crest Trail: This famous footpath, now pre-empted by the Angeles Crest Highway, crossed the backbone of the mountains from Chilao to Islip Saddle, then down the North Fork of the San Gabriel River to Coldwater Camp. A branch went from Islip Saddle down the South Fork of Big Rock Creek to the old Shoemaker Ranger Station. Hunters, anglers, and adventurers traveled it in great numbers from the 1890s into the 1930s. Today, parts are gone completely, and other parts parallel the Angeles Crest Highway a few hundred feet above.

Azusa-Camp Rincon Trail: When the San Gabriel River flooded in the old days, travel up the main canyon was virtually impossible. When this happened, visitors to Camp Rincon—a popular resort located where the present Rincon Ranger Station stands—took the "high road" over the mountains west of the river. Today the lower part of the old pathway is still passable; the upper section has been pre-empted by the Red Box-Rincon fire road.

Bighorn Ridge-Old Baldy Trail: In the early decades of the century, Weber's Camp in Coldwater Canyon, a tributary of the East Fork of the San Gabriel River, was a popular trail resort. A trail was built from the camp up massive Bighorn Ridge to the summit of Baldy. With the demise of Weber's Camp in the '20s, the trail was abandoned. It has now virtually disappeared.

San Dimas Canyon Trail: San Dimas Canyon is now part of the San Dimas Experimental Forest, where various types of conifers are tested to determine their suitability to the Southern California mountains. Trails in and around the canyon are closed to the public.

Lookout Mountain Trail: In 1913 the first fire-lookout tower in Angeles National Forest was built, atop Lookout Mountain, which is a bump on Baldy's great south ridge. A trail was constructed from Camp Baldy to Bear Flat, then up to the summit. It became a favorite of Camp Baldy visitors because of the superb panorama available from Lookout Mountain. In 1927 the lookout was moved to nearby Sunset Peak and the trail was abandoned. Today it has disappeared in the chaparral. You can climb Lookout Mountain today from the Glendora Mountain Road at Cow Canyon Saddle, utilizing a narrow trail and the fire break.

Bibliography

Nature

Booth, Ernest S., *Mammals of Southern California*, U. of Calif. Press, Berkeley, 1968

Dawson, E. Yale, *Cacti of California*, U. of Calif. Press, Berkeley, 1966

DeLisle, Harold, *Common Plants of the Southern California Mountains*, Naturegraph Co., Healdsburg, 1961

DeLisle, Harold, *Wildlife of the Southern California Mountains*, Naturegraph Co., Healdsburg, 1963

Munz, Philip, and David Keck, *California Mountain Wildflowers*, U. of Calif. Press, Berkeley, 1968

Peterson, P. Victor, *Native Trees of Southern California*, U. of Calif. Press, Berkeley, 1966

Raven, Peter H., *Native Shrubs of Southern California*, U. of Calif. Press, Berkeley, 1966

Sudworth, George, *Forest Trees of the Pacific Slope*, Dover Publications, New York, 1967

Trent, D. D., "Mount Baldy Mining Area" *California Geology*, August 1986.

History

Johnson, Bernice E., *California's Gabrielino Indians*, Southwest Museum, Los Angeles, 1962

Johnson, Frank, *The Serrano Indians of Southern California*, Malki Museum Press, Banning, 1965

Owens, Glen, *The Heritage of Big Santa Anita*, Big Santa Anita Historical Society, Arcadia, CA, 1981

Robinson, John W., *Mines of the Salt Gabriels*, La Siesta Press, Glendale, 1973

_____, *The San Gabriels: The Mountain Country from Soledad Canyon to Lytle Creek*, Big Santa Anita Historical Society, Arcadia, CA, 1991

Robinson, W. W., *The Forest and The People: The Story of Angeles National Forest*, Title Insurance & Trust Co., Los Angeles, 1946.

Saunders, Charles F., *The Southern Sierras of California*, Houghton Mifflin Co., Boston, 1923 (out of print)

Sargent, Shirley, *Theodore Parker Lukens: Father of Forestry*, Dawson's Book Shop, Los Angeles, 1969

Seims, Charles, *Mount Lowe: The Railway in the Clouds*, Golden West Books, San Marine, CA, 1976

Thrall, Will (ed.), *Trails* magazine, L.A. County Dept. of Recr. Camps &
   Playgrounds, Los Angeles, 1934-39 (2 issues 1941)
Vernon, Charles C., *A History of the San Gabriel Mountains*, Southern
   California Quarterly, 4 issues, 1956

Index